# GARDEN OF MYSTERY

CLASSICS OF SUFI POETRY

No. 2

# GARDEN OF MYSTERY

## The Gulshan-i rāz
### of
### Mahmud Shabistari

Translated by
ROBERT ABDUL HAYY DARR

Published by
ARCHETYPE
Chetwynd House, Bartlow, Cambridge CB21 4PP, UK
First published in 2007, reprinted in 2020.

ISBN 10:  1 901383 21 0 (cloth)
ISBN 13:  978 1 901383 21 8 (cloth)

ISBN 10:  1 901383 22 9 (pb)
ISBN 13:  978 1 901383 22 5 (pb)

A full CIP record for this book is available from
The British Library.

Typography by Robert Bringhurst Ltd.
The types in this book are *Poetica* and *Garamond Premier,*
designed in San Jose, California, by Robert Slimbach;
Decotype *Naskh,* created in Amsterdam by
Thomas Milo *&* Mirjam Somers; CRULP *Nafees Nastaleeq,*
designed in Lahore by Jamil ur-Rehman, based on the hand
of his teacher Nafees al-Hussaini (1933–2008);
and Microsoft's تنضيد الحروف العربية ("Arabic Typesetting"),
designed in Seattle and Vancouver by Mamoun Sakkal,
Paul C. Nelson, *&* John Hudson.

# ∾ CONTENTS ∾

The *Garden of Mystery* [*Gulshan-i rāz*] is a basic text for Persian-speaking followers of the Sufi tradition, the mystical dimension of Islam. It is a poem of about one thousand rhyming couplets, which addresses the essential concerns of the Sufi way with great precision and eloquence.

It was composed by Sa'd al-Din Mahmud Shabistari, who was born at Shabistar, near Tabriz, Iran, about 1288 and who died there in 1339. Shabistari was a well-known Sufi in the area who lived at a time of great change following the Mongol invasions that devastated all of Central Asia. This branch of the Mongols, later named the Il-Khanids, had made Tabriz its capital some years before the writing of the *Gulshan-i rāz*. In Shabistari's lifetime, Tabriz was a major center of government, commerce, and learning. Before their conversion to Islam, the Il-Khanids were Buddhists and Shamanists. They invited Buddhist teachers from India and Tibet to establish themselves in Tabriz. These Mongols also allied themselves with the Christians and Jews until the reign of the monarch Abu Sa'id who, under the influence of narrow-minded Muslim clerics, had churches and synagogues destroyed and the Buddhists expelled from the region. It was in the liberal atmosphere characterized by religious diversity at the beginning of the fourteenth century that the *Gulshan-i rāz* was composed. The *Gulshan-i rāz* takes the form of a series of questions and replies. Shabistari informs us that the questions originated with Shaikh Sayyid Husseini of Khorasan (in what is now Herat, Afghanistan), and were presented to the assembly of Sufis to which Shabistari belonged.

The early fourteenth century was a golden age for Sufism despite the unparalleled social and political turmoil of the times. If anything, the slaughter and destruction wrought by the Mongols demonstrated the impermanence of worldly existence and guided many to seek spiritual illumination. A number of Sufi orders survived and helped with the re-establishment of farming, education and other social structures. Dervishes (followers of the Sufi way) spent time in the service of humanity as well as in prayer and inner exercises such as the remembrance of God and meditation. Travel was another Sufi method of broadening the minds and refining the character of dervishes. Travel also resulted in a cross-pollination of ideas and practices from the various schools of Sufism from Spain to China and probably some contact with other mystical traditions.

The greatest literary influence on Shabistari was the Koran, for Muslims the word of God, revealed to the Prophet Muhammad through God's angel Gabriel. The Koran establishes the relationships between God and creation through the revelation of statements, stories (including many familiar to Jews and Christians), questions, arguments and admonishments. The Arabic of the Koran is compelling and poetic, enlivening the text's meanings; translations of it often seem dry and harsh in contrast. Shabistari quotes it frequently to support or illustrate his spiritual messages. Related to the Koran are the *ḥadīths* or sayings concerning the Prophet Muhammad. Some of these are called *qudsī* or 'sacred,' since they are considered to be extra-Koranic inspirations from God. Other *ḥadīths* are observations that Muhammad made or anecdotes about him that were recorded by his closest followers. It is from a radically unitarian Islamic perspective that Shabistari investigates and describes mystical experience. He denies notions of incarnation or true union with God for the mystic, a theme often found in the mysticism of India. He denies free will in mankind, regarding which he had doubtless considered the views of the Zoroastrians, Christians, and certain factions within Islam. Finally, he opposes any notion of sorcery, personal power or independence in the mystic way.

In his introduction, Shabistari extols the poetic works of Farīd al-Dīn ʿAṭṭār, the great Khorasani poet (died 1229) who was also a great influence on Jalal al-Din Rumi. Although there is no discernable influence of ʿAṭṭār's style in the poetry of the *Gulshan-i rāz,* it is clear that Persian Sufism, with its wide use of symbolic imagery in expressing the love of God, was a major influence in Shabistari's work. This is especially apparent in the last five inquiries of the *Gulshan-i rāz.*

The *Gulshan-i rāz* abounds with evidence of Shabistari's exposure to the works of such Muslim interpreters of Greek philosophy as Ibn Sina, al-Kindi, al-Farabi, and the mystic Ibn al-ʿArabi. The works of Plato, Aristotle, Plotinus and other neoplatonists were absorbed and partly modified by the thinkers of Islam, who felt the need to add an intellectual and philosophical interpretation to the more devotional approach of the Koran. This eventually led to a most interesting cosmology. For Shabistari, the most useful synthesis of Islam and Greek thought was found in the writings of the Andalusian Sufi, Ibn al-ʿArabi. The influence of his thought permeates the *Gulshan-i rāz*, in particular, his vast exegesis on the Sufi concept of the "oneness of Being" [*waḥdat al-wujūd*]. Shabistari seems also to have been greatly influenced by the great Sufi and "Proof of Islam," Abu Hamid al-Ghazali who loosened the hold of Greek philosophy on the Islamic culture of his time. Shabistari joins him in reproaching Muslim philosophers whom he sees as intellectually playing with Greek thought rather than experiencing the spiritual Reality referred to in their writings.

A number of doctrinal disputes affected the study of Sufism in Shabistari's time. The most serious were between Sufis and literalist Muslims, but differences also existed between Sufis and the philosophers and members of other creeds. The Sufis had become a threat to the literalists a few centuries earlier because of Sufi insistence on personal, experiential contact with the Divine. Sufi experience often led to ecstatic utterances which were at odds with the literalist religious view and, because of this, a number of mystics were put to death. The most famous case was that of Mansur al-Hallaj, who publicly made the claim, "I am the Divine Reality" [*ana al-ḥaqq*] a statement that led to his violent execution by the Abbasid authorities in Baghdad in 922 AD.

Opposition to al-Hallaj came not only from the literalists, but also from many 'sober' Sufis, including the influential al-Junayd of Baghdad. In the case of the theologians, this was because they could not accept any religious experience that did not accord with a narrow exoteric reading of the Koran. Certain Sufis opposed Hallaj's divulgence of spiritual realities which, although true, might jeopardize the terrestrial religious law needed by most people to maintain social order. Shabistari handles these theological difficulties clearly, using the arguments of the earlier Sufis, especially their conception of the 'oneness of Being' [*waḥdat al-wujūd*]. *Wujūd* may be translated as 'being' or 'existence,' inferred from its root meaning of 'finding.' *Wajd* and *wajdan,* meaning 'ecstasy' and 'mystical consciousness,' are also from this root. When Shabistari uses words for existence and being in his poem, he does so with the understanding that they are related to substantive experiential states and are not merely ontological descriptions. *Waḥdat al-wujūd* is an Islamic doctrine with striking similarities to concepts found in Taoism, and the Advaita (non-duality) school of Hinduism. Yet its supporters use statements from the Koran for its basis, and claim that this Reality must be experienced by the mystic. Though attacked as pantheistic, the doctrine is much more complex and has remained a central focus of the Sufis for the last seven hundred years. Through it, Shabistari defends al-Hallaj as someone who has purified his conscious-ness of *self-identity,* leaving room for the Divine to speak, "I am the Divine Reality."

A common theme running through the *Gulshan-i rāz* is the illusory nature of our usual experience and of our existence. In Shabistari's time, as in our own, there were doctrines that stated that an individual could determine his or her own fate or that through personal power, one could perform magic or achieve some sort of partnership with the Divine. Shabistari explains these doctrines as delusions of the *self,* the barrier to understanding the human's place within the *oneness of Being.* Personal identity in the form of the self is considered by Sufis to distort reality be-cause of its attachment to the objects of this world and because of the acceptance of personality, and its desires, as one's real identity. From infancy to adult-hood, the trap of unreal self-notion becomes ever tight-er, and is reinforced constantly through a mentality whose *modus operandi* is automatism, self-defense, self-aggrandizement and delusion. The Sufi has bro-ken through this trap, removed the bonds that inhibit perception and cleansed the impurities of the self to allow a greater influence from the Real to manifest in his spiritual 'heart.' According to Shabistari, the human destiny is the transcending of the hypocrisy of *self* and the expanding of the spiritual *heart* which, when purified, becomes a mirror in which the Real expresses and knows Itself. The Sufi who achieves this goal becomes a microcosm of the Real and is named the Completed Human Being (*insān-i kāmil*).

The reader will notice that the later chapters of the *Gulshan-i rāz* are of a different literary style that is more symbolic and ecstatic in character. These chapters concern themselves more with Sufi experience and less with its doctrine. The first few questions, on the other hand, establish the philosophical and cosmological doctrines current in Shabistari's time, especially those which were developed by Ibn al-'Arabi.[1] In truth, one cannot approach a deep understanding of the *Gulshan-i rāz* without having made some study of Ibn al-'Arabi. His conceptions of God as harmoniously immanent *and* transcendent, unknown to mankind yet ever-present and personal, beyond creation while simultaneously creation itself, seem contradictory but are basic to Sufi experience and doctrine. Also confusing to some is Ibn

---

1 For a better understanding of Ibn al-'Arabi's doctrines, I recommend reading William C. Chittick's *The Sufi Path of Knowledge* (Albany, New York: SUNY Press, 1989) and R.W.J. Austin's *Ibn al-'Arabi: The Bezels of Wisdom* (New York: Paulist Press, 1980).

al-ʿArabi's notion of creation as real yet not real. It is not real because it is an illusion, like the projection of film from a movie projector.

In this simile, what is seen is actually God's light shining through the film of every individual's essential archetype (called collectively the *aʿyān thābita,* which remain forever unmanifested in God's Self-knowledge) and projected onto the screen of relative existence. From this unusual point of view, it is absurd for a person to imagine that he or she has any real existence or free will. Yet creation is also real, precisely because it is the action of God in the realm of the *contingent,* a shadow-play world where light and darkness, existence and nonexistence meet and interact. There are innumerable plots in this shadow play but only one underlying theme. This theme is reflected in the important *ḥadīth,* "I was a hidden treasure and I longed to be known. I created the cosmos so that I would be known."

The *Gulshan-i rāz* has been held in such esteem in the Islamic world that dozens of commentaries were written by various Sufis to explain its mystery and complexity. The most famous and trustworthy commentary, written by Muhammad Lahiji, is itself a major work several times longer than the *Gulshan-i rāz,* giving a paragraph of exegesis for each couplet. Of this work, Toshihiko Izutsu has written, "The importance of the *Garden of Mystery* has induced a number of distinguished thinkers to write commentaries upon it, the most important of which is the *Mafātīḥ al-iʿjāz fī sharḥ Gulshan-i rāz* by Lahiji.... His commentary has been studied for centuries not only as the best commentary upon the *Garden of Mystery,* but also as one of the most lucid, systematic expositions of Sufi philosophy written in Persian."[2]

The first Western translation of the *Gulshan-i rāz* consisted of extracts published by the German orientalist Friedrich Tholuck, in 1825. Since then a number of translations into European languages have appeared, several of them in English. A fine translation into French was made in 1991 by Jamshid Mortazavi and Eva de Vitray-Meyerovitch, *La Roseraie du mystère.* In 1995, Dr. Leonard Lewisohn published a definitive work on Shabistari's life and teachings, *Beyond Faith and Infidelity: the Sufi Poetry and Teachings of Mahmud Shabistari.*[3]

Mahmud Shabistari is also the author of several less known works. These are 'The Truth of Certainty' [*Ḥaqq al-Yaqīn*]; 'The Book of Joy' [*Saʿadat Nameh*]; and 'The Book of the Witness' [*Shāhid Nameh*].

The *Gulshan-i rāz* deserves special attention from students of Sufism because it is one of the most important classical works in Persian. In the present version I have avoided rhyming verse which, although

---

2 Toshihiko Izutsu, *Creation and the Timeless Order of Things* (Ashland, Oregon: White Cloud Press, 1994), p 39.

3 London: Curzon Press, 1995; 2nd ed., UCI Jordan Center for Persian Studies, Irvine, California, 2020.

lovely in the original, does not suit today's audience. I have capitalized all words that refer to God or the Real even though capitalization does not appear in Arabic/Persian script. Persian is gender neutral. This immediately gives rise to a complication for English translation. I have resolved this difficulty by translating the he/she/it pronoun *"u"* as *he* (as is the problematic convention), but occasionally I have deviated from this, using she and occasionally it. Bracketed words are additions that I have used to clarify an occasionally ambiguous verse. My translation was made from the Persian using Samad Muwahhid's critical edition of the *Gulshan-i rāz,* and taking into account five earlier translations and Muhammad Lahiji's commentary. It should be noted that Muwahhid's edition, made using the oldest and most genuine manuscripts available, has corrected a fair number of variant couplets from later manuscripts of the *Gulshan-i rāz,* including many verses commented upon by Lahiji.

## ❧ ACKNOWLEDGMENTS ❧

I must express my deep and abiding gratitude to all who have helped me with this project. I thank Alan Godlas, Herbert Mason and Seyyed Hossein Nasr for their early encouragement, and especially Leonard Lewisohn, who tirelessly gave generous attention and constructive criticism to my work. I would also like to express my gratitude to all of the earlier translators from whom I learned. The reward found in the labor of translation is to be able to contemplate a special, meaningful work of art very slowly and carefully, digesting it as one goes along. Yet there is frustration of knowing that one cannot match the original poetic language. Nevertheless, my hope is that sincere and patient readers will benefit from this translation, and overlook the difficulties inherent in translating mystical poetry.

# گلشنِ راز

سعدالدین محمود شبستری

# GARDEN OF MYSTERY

(*Gulshan-i rāz*)

Mahmud Shabistari introduces this profound classic on spirituality by summarizing mankind's predicament and the need for spiritual guidance. The human condition is such that we experience the world and life as chaotic and inexplicable because we are cut off from the underlying unity and source of all things. The truth that most people do not feel is that all phenomena and their relations are manifestations of divine unitary Being. We have created an illusion of separateness, a mental construct [*amr i'tibārī*] through our physical senses, and our mental and emotional attachments. Spirituality is the means to return to our real nature, grounded in the spirit abiding in each individual. Prophets and saints are those who are chosen by God for the task of guiding humanity back to its origin in Being. The Prophet Muhammad is considered the archetype of prophecy, perfect in spirituality, so his spirit guides all of creation from the beginning to the end of historical time. Saints are those individuals who are friends of God. Shabistari summarizes the variety of their presentations that accord with their individual predispositions.

Next, Shabistari gives his reasons for writing the *Gulshan-i rāz*. He mentions a great Sufi by the name of Sayyid Husseini who has sent from Khorasan a broad range of questions covering much of Islamic spirituality. Shabistari is asked by fellow Sufis to answer the questions and he is later asked to compile the whole as a book of poetry. He claims to have composed the *Gulshan-i rāz* in a matter of hours. Although on the face of it, this might seem like an improbable boast, it should be kept in mind that Sufis usually did produce great literature during short periods of ecstatic consciousness. This allowed them to externalize to some degree the depths of spiritual knowledge that they held in their hearts. That is the manner in which both Rumi and Ibn al-ʿArabi composed their own works that were much longer than Shabistari's compositions. Shabistari's unique genius is in the distillation of meaning. His verses strike aphoristic flashes of gnostic lightning in the reader's mind, yet retain continuity in meaning through each discourse.

Shabistari adds the caveat both in his introduction and elsewhere that these words cannot be truly understood by the uninitiated. The intention of the work is to give a basic understanding of the Sufi approach so that seekers of God can proceed to cultivate those spiritual states which alone confer a deep understanding of such words.

بِسْمِ اللَّهِ الرَّحْمَنِ الرَّحِيمِ

اب کنت ثب

بم نے

و

بِسْمِ اللَّهِ الرَّحْمَنِ الرَّحِيمِ

*In the name of Allah, the Compassionate, the Merciful*

In the name of the One who inspired the soul to contemplate;
Who kindled the lamp of the Heart with the light of Spirit.

The two worlds were illumined by His favor.
Through His bounty, Adam's clay was a garden of flowers.

The Powerful One in a wink of the eye, with the letters
forming BE!, made to appear both of the worlds.

When the P of His power breathed onto the Pen,
thousands of images filled the tablet of nonbeing.

From that Breath the two worlds came into existence.                5
From that very Breath appeared the soul of Adam.

Discernment manifested in Adam through reason
so that he might come to know the source of all things.

When he came to see himself as a separate individual,
he reflected on the question "What am I?"

He made the long journey from the part to the All
and returned from there to view the world's existence.

He now saw the world as a fictitious manifestation,
like 'one' diffused through the many numbers.

10    The material and spiritual worlds sprang from one Breath,
coming into and departing existence in that same Breath.

Yet this isn't a situation of coming and going.
When observed aright, going isn't other than coming.

Things revert to their proper origin.
The hidden and apparent become one thing.

God Most High, the Ancient, made in one breath
the beginning and conclusion of both worlds.

The material and spiritual worlds here become one.
One becomes many and is again reduced [by unification].

15    All this illusion of otherness springs from your fancy,
for the point looks a circle by the speed it's spun.

It is but a circle's line from beginning to end
upon which journeys all the world's creation.

On this path are the prophets who are guides.
They are leaders and directors of the caravan.

Of them, our Prince [Muḥammad] became the chief,
the first and the very last in prophecy.

Aḥad [the One] in the M of Aḥmad became manifest.
In this circle, the first is the same as the last.

With him this road is concluded and sealed.                    20
To him was revealed to "call you to God."

His heart-expanding station is all-comprehensive unity;
His soul-enlivening beauty is the candle of gatherings.

He has gone ahead and all other souls follow him;
All souls clutch the hem of his robe for guidance.

The many friends of God on this road, present and past,
have given signs of their states and attainments.

Having reached the capacity of their own awareness,
each spoke of the divine Known and the human knower.

One from within the Ocean of Unity said, "I am the Real!"    25
One spoke of the earthly vessel's nearness and distance.

Another, having mastered exoteric knowledge,
gave signs of the dryness of the shore.

One dared to expose the Pearl, thus becoming a target,
while another left the Pearl aside to consider the shell.

One spoke openly about the parts and the Whole.
Another referred to the temporal and the Eternal.

One alluded to 'curl,' 'beauty-mark,' and 'facial down,'
and explained it with 'wine,' 'candle,' and 'Witness.'

30    Since each explained things according to his own station,
people have found it difficult to understand the matter.

Whoever is yet bewildered by the inner meaning
is in need of trying to understand it.

## ⁓ THE REASON ⁓
## ⁓ FOR WRITING THIS BOOK ⁓

Seven hundred and seventeen years had elapsed
since the Hejira when suddenly in the month of Shawwal,

a messenger endowed with a thousand graces and virtues
arrived here from the learned society of Khorasan.

In Khorasan lived a great man of renown
whose many graces were like a fountain of light.

35    All of the people of Khorasan, great and small,
said that he stood supreme in this epoch.

He was the joy of the world and a light of the soul,
this leader of the mystics, Sayyid Husseini.

He had written a letter concerning spiritual meaning
which he sent to the masters of spirituality.

Within the letter were many difficult expressions
used by the masters of symbolic allusion.

He had arranged in verse a series of questions,
each a world of meaning within a few words.

The messenger read the letter to those present                    40
and surprised silence fell over the assembly.

The friends of that assembly became interested
and turned their attention toward this humble dervish.

One of the most accomplished adepts of the Path
who had often heard me speak of these subtleties

said to me, "Give these questions answers now
since there is benefit in this for everyone."

I replied to him, "What need is there?
I've already dealt with such questions in treatises."

"That's so, but regarding these questions," he said,              45
"I want to hear you answer them in verse."

Because of his entreaty, I began to recite.
I answered the letter neatly and concisely.

Suddenly, I recited to this circle of liberated souls,
speaking without thinking or repeating myself.

I said, "By your grace and charity,
please overlook my faults."

"Everyone knows that I've not in my life
used poetry to express myself."

50  "Though I am naturally gifted with words,
I've only rarely recited poetry."

"I've indeed written books of prose,
but not busied myself with a mathnawi."

"Meter and rhyme can't measure inner meaning.
Not every container can hold spirit's meaning."

"Inner meaning is not found in words
any more than the Red Sea is held in a cup."

"By using words I'm already in difficult straits.
Why increase the difficulty by stringing verse?"

55  "These words are not a boast, but said in gratitude
and apology to the people of heart-feeling."

"I'll not be disgraced for writing poetry since
another ʿAṭṭār won't appear in a hundred centuries."

"The literary airs and graces of a hundred hidden worlds
would equal but one brief passage in the Diwan of ʿAṭṭār."

"But this comes through occasional grace,
not from snatching angels' words like demons."

Eventually, I answered the letter's questions
and wrote them out one by one, no more nor less.

The messenger respectfully took the replies                    60
and returned home on the same road.

Later, the friend who requested replies
asked me to expand further on them.

"Unveil the inner meanings of this matter.
Make the essence of this gnosis truly clear."

I hadn't the chance in those moments of rapture
to convey the inner 'taste' of my spiritual state.

It's impossible to describe such experiences in words,
and only the adepts of mystical states know these states.

Yet by the counsel of the founder of our Faith,                 65
I could not deny this sincere inquirer's petition.

So I set out to make these secrets more clear
and the parrot of eloquence burst into speech.

With God's grace and help guiding me to success,
I was able to deliver the whole thing in a few hours.

My heart asked the Divine Presence to name the work.
The reply came to my heart that "This is Our Garden."

Since His Presence has named this book the "Garden,"
may He forever illuminate the eyes of all hearts.

In Shabistari's own introduction to the *Garden of Mystery,* he notes that the questions at the center of the work were composed by Mir Sayyid Husseini, a highly accomplished mystic. Thus Husseini's questions reference themes that he considered significant in the study of mysticism.

The first question he poses concerns thought and reflection [*fikr* and *tafakkur*], issues which were important in Sufi practice as well as in the theology and philosophy of the time. Shabistari immediately presents a Sufi definition:

> *Reflection is going from the false toward the Real,*
> *To behold within the part the Absolute Whole.*

Shabistari then contrasts this to the more conventional Islamic view of reflection derived from the Greek philosophers. In this approach, reflection begins with a reminiscence [*anamnesis*], which initially presents itself as a mental concept. Applying Aristotelian logic, this concept becomes a major premise which, when combined with a minor premise, allows one to arrive at an interpretation of its meaning.

Shabistari examines this approach, and points out its inherent limitations in discovering Reality directly. First, such an encounter requires divine assistance. Moreover, true reflection occurs in a mind abstracted from the world of form, which can then witness all things through the unity of their essential origin. On the other hand, when the mind seeks the truth but never transcends itself, it is

[ 33 ]

unable truly to know itself and the universe. Such a mind he compares to a fool wandering in the desert with a candle seeking the brilliant sun.

Philosophy looks at phenomena and attempts to derive their origins. Shabistari points out that "The manifested appearance of all things is by opposites/But the Real has neither like nor opposite." In other words, the essential Source of the world of forms is completely different from the usual categories of physical and mental phenomena that always have some frame of reference. Yet the Source is within all things, in one sense it is all things, for he claims,

> *Know the whole world as the glare of the Real's light;*
> *The Real is concealed in it through obviousness.*

For Shabistari, true reflection is only possible for someone who has experienced mystical unveiling [*kashf*], and who finds that this reflection begins and ends with its source in God. Any other method of investigation involves speculation and imitation, both of which are subject to error.

First of all, I am perplexed by my own thought.          70
What is it that's referred to as 'reflection'?

∾ REPLY ∾

You've asked me, "What is reflection?"
since you're perplexed about its meaning.

Reflection is going from the false toward the Real,
to behold within the part the Absolute Whole.

Philosophers who've written treatises on this topic
have said the following when describing this process:

When a conception manifests in the heart,
it is initially termed a recollection.

After thinking about it for a time,                      75
it's commonly called an interpretation.

The conception thus pondered and ordered
is what the logicians describe as reflection.

By arranging well-understood conceptions,
you can ascertain the unknown from the known.

The major premise is like a father, the minor a mother;
What is the result? A child, O brother.

But the ordering of logic's parameters
necessarily employs the rules of logic.

80 In any case, if not done with divine assistance,
such reflection is only blind imitation.

That road is long and arduous so leave it now.
Like Moses for a moment, put down your staff.

Come for a while into the Valley of Peace.
Hear "Truly, I am God" without any doubt.

For the gnostic witnessing Unity
what's first seen? It's the light of Being.

A heart that is illuminated by gnosis
sees God first in anything it looks upon.

85 True thought requires abstraction [from self].
Then shines the radiant light of His grace.

Whoever's not shown along this way by God
will have nothing disclosed by the use of logic.

Since the doctor of philosophy is in perplexity,
he can't see anything in creation but contingent being.

[ 36 ]

From the contingent he tries to prove the Necessary,
so he remains perplexed about the Essence of God.

Sometimes he travels backwards in a vicious circle.
Sometimes he is shackled by chains of logical proofs.

As his mind ponders over phenomenal existence, 90
his feet trip up in logical proofs.

The appearance of all things is by contraries,
but the Real has neither likeness nor contrary.

Since his Essence has no likeness nor contrary,
I don't know how you'll come to know Him.

The contingent world has no sample of the Necessary;
how then can one understand It, how?

Alas, the fool who for the sake of the brilliant sun
wanders the desert seeking it by the light of a candle.

 ILLUSTRATION

If the sun remained in one stationary condition, 95
its rays would be emitted from one direction.

A person would not realize that these were sun's rays
or know the difference between the kernel and the husk.

Know the whole world as the glare of the Real's light.
The Real is concealed in it through obviousness.

The light of the Real does not shift and alter.
Its Essence has no change nor permutation.

You imagine the world itself is constant and unchanging,
that it endures through its own essential nature.

100 The person whose intellect strays far and wide
will find himself bewildered in the searching.

From the mischievous intellect's straying,
one's a philosopher, another an incarnationist.

Reason cannot bear the light of that Face.
For its sake, go find a different pair of eyes.

The philosopher's eyes, squinting with double vision,
are barred from seeing the unity of the Real.

Comparisons of God arise from blindness.
One-eyed sight results in transcendental perspectives.

105 Transmigration of souls is but vain heresy
since it is the product of near-sightedness.

Like one born blind, deprived of perfection,
is he who goes the way of the Rationalists.

The externalists rub their diseased eyes in pain.
In the outer world they see only its manifestations.

The theologian who is devoid of the 'taste' of Unity
is plunged in darkness, enveloped in clouds of imitation.

Whatever each may say from such perspectives
reveals the limitation of his own vision.

His Essence remains free of how, what, or how much.          110
The High and Sublime Essence is above what men say.

This rather long section extends the first inquiry into the nature of reflection. In his answer to this inquiry, Shabistari looks at the limitations of the thought process and then at its usefulness. He points out that it is not possible to know the Essence of God through thinking. Indeed, it is a transgression to do so. The Real is everywhere, he says, and is the basis of the apparent world. As such, it is hidden both from direct observation and from thought. The way to direct, experiential understanding is to "leave aside your intellect and be ever with the Real," and to "know it's impossible to gain what you already have." In other words, what you already have as your own essential basis is the Real within you. To become aware of this, you must transcend the phenomenal world and the process of reflection itself. As consciousness approaches the presence of the Real the finite personality is overwhelmed, just as "when an object is brought up close to the eye, vision is obscured in trying to see it."

The Real is so brilliant that human reason is extinguished in It. Shabistari writes that "Reason's light is to the luminous Essence like the light of the eye dazed by the sun." This leads to an experience of the "black light of the Essence," which is the blacking out of individual perception in the presence of Divine Perception. It is, however, possible to experience the Real as reflected in the human consciousness, just as "though human eyes cannot withstand its brilliance, it is possible to observe the sun reflected on water." This simile refers to observing the Real's action on nonbeing. By nonbeing is meant the immutable entities [al-aʿyān al-thābita], the essences of all things which are called nonbeing because they have no empirical existence of their own but abide immutably in the Real's knowledge.

An understanding of the immutable entities must include a consideration of the nature of delimitation. Since Divinity is, in Its absoluteness, beyond any delimitation whatsoever, divine knowledge of the entities is knowledge of the delimitation of absoluteness. This is an ontological necessity known as 'differentiation,' one that occurs in the formation of universal archetypes [umūr kulliyya] and as the individual entities. Yet the Real is so unlimited that It is not limited from having determinations or limitations on its Absoluteness. These limitations are the expressions or manifestations of pure Being, all reflecting the supreme Identity, which of Itself has no description.

Thus any entity in the visible and invisible universe is known to the Divine as a restriction of Itself, no matter how beautiful or how ugly it seems to the human mind. The Real gives a relative existence to these immutable entities by acting upon them through a number of divine relational attributes known as the Divine Names. Each of the empirically nonexistent immutable entities, however simple or complex, has predispositions or latencies, which can come to expression only through the activity of one of these 'Names' of the Real. Thus the Name al-Baṣīr, the Seeing, acts on the latency in creatures to manifest the range of vision existing in nature.

In summary, Self-delimitation and differentiation originate within the Essential Self-articulation. The intention of this differentiation may be found in the *ḥadīth qudsī* (extra-Koranic revelation): "I was a hidden treasure and I longed to be known. I created the cosmos so that I would be known."

Coming back to the point that "It is possible to observe the sun reflected on water," we should remember that this observation takes place within the heart and in the world. The Koranic verse, "We will show them Our signs on the horizons and within their souls until it becomes clear that He is the Real," (Koran 41:53) is much quoted by Sufis to emphasize this point. The signs shown "within their souls" are sought through the contemplative disciplines of mysticism. The signs found within are increasingly refined theophanies which eventually move beyond sensation, thought, and imagination, to a pure, ineffable experience of the Real. In this connection, Shabistari writes, "Nonbeing is a mirror, the world its image. Man is the eye of this image beholding the hidden Essence," a concept which he borrows from Ibn al-ʿArabi's *Fuṣūṣ al-ḥikam*.

Shabistari connects the original topic, "which of my thoughts are a condition of the path?" with the first half of the Koranic verse (41:53): "We will show them Our signs on the horizons." This topic concerns another specialization of the Sufi Way which is *fikr,* thinking about God's actions in the world around us. Shabistari devotes most of this chapter to his particular approach to *fikr.* The exercise of *fikr* is complementary to *dhikr,* the invocation of Allah's name. When correctly learned and practiced, *dhikr* leads to *kashf,* or mystical unveiling, and to a mystical certainty of God's presence and mercy. *Fikr* initially allows the seeker to develop gratitude toward God for His mercies, and to experience awe for the vast complexity of God's creation. At a higher spiritual stage, when *dhikr* has had its effects, the seeker sees all things around him as *āyāt,* 'signs' of God, which correspond to the verses of the Koran, also called *āyāt.* The world becomes a manifestation of the holy book and all of its contents, and events become spiritually relevant signs from God.

In this section of the inquiry, Shabistari guides our own reflection with his interpretation of Koranic verses, which correspond to Sufi cosmology. His exegesis considers the descent of Being from the Universal Intellect and Universal Soul, to the level of the physical cosmos, here understood as the Ptolemaic spheres. Finally, there is the level of terrestrial existence, which is outwardly a synthesis of the four elements. Inwardly, the soul of humanity encompasses all of the levels of this descent, and can transcend them to return to pure Being. This process is regarded as a journey [*sayr u suluk*], which first takes the spiritual pilgrim into the visionary realms of the Imaginal World ['*ālam al-mithāl*].

All people have limited personal experience of the Imaginal World through dreams and fantasies, which are its microcosmic representations. The Imaginal World is the manifestation of the immutable entities of the cosmos as seen in the comprehensive Divine dream. This is an intermediary world joining the sensible with the intelligible. A fair portion of all Sufi literature concerns itself with visions from this realm, achieved through meditation and detachment from the bodily senses.

Shabistari closes this inquiry with an examination of the relational attributes of the Real called the Names. He says:

> *All beings have secured existence through a Name;*
> *By that Name they are continually worshipping the Real.*

Every creature's existence can be traced to the action of a Name. It is possible for human beings to assume and reflect all of the Names. What defines the Perfect Human is that he or she is the comprehensive locus of all the Names, a mirror of the named, *Allah*. Behind the qualities of the Names is their Essential Reality, unique and without quality. The spiritual heart of the Perfect Human is considered to be the only manifestation in the cosmos able to 'contain' the Divine Unity.

Which reflection is a necessary condition of the Way?
Why is thought sometimes worship and sometimes sin?


∾ REPLY ∾

Reflecting on God's many blessings is a condition
but reflecting on the Essence of the Real is transgression.

Reflecting on God's Essence is completely vain.
Know it's impossible to gain what one has.

While worldly signs are illuminated by the Essence,
the Essence is not illuminated through these signs.

All of the world has appeared by His Light                    115
yet how can He be revealed through the world?

The Essential Light is not in the manifestations.
Its glorious Majesty would devastate them.

Let go of your intellect and be with the Real.
A bat's eye cannot bear the sun's brilliance.

In that state where the Real's light proves itself,
what room is there for Angel Gabriel's speech?

Though a lofty angel is near the Divine Court,
he can't reach the state of "I have a time with God."

120  As that Light burns even a pure angel's wings,
it would scorch the whole of reason head to foot.

Reason's light is to the luminous Essence
like the light of the eye dazed by the sun.

When an object is brought up close to the eye,
sight grows dark in trying to perceive it.

Blackness, if you but knew, is the Light of the Essence;
Within the darkness flows the Water of Life.

Blackness absorbs the eye's weak light.
Abandon vision since this isn't its place.

125  What relationship has dust to the Pure World?
Comprehension lies in the lapse of comprehension.

Never shall the black face [of nonbeing] be separated
from creatures in either world; "God's the best Knower."

The dervish's "black face in the two worlds"
reaches the all-comprehensive Supreme Darkness.

What can I say about this most subtle secret
of a luminous night within a dark day?

[ 46 ]

In *this revelation which is luminous theophany,*
*I have many words but silence is better.*

*If you want to view the sun's bright source,*                    130
*you'll have to see it on an intermediary surface.*

*Though human eyes can't bear this brilliance,*
*they can view the sun reflected on water.*

*Since the sun's brilliance is here diminished*
*your perception of it can be maintained.*

*Nonbeing is the mirror of Absolute Being.*
*The Real's brilliant reflection appears in it.*

*When nonbeing became aligned opposite Being,*
*a reflection then occurred in nonbeing.*

*Unity became visible from this multiplicity.*                    135
*The number one when counted became many.*

*Although numbers all begin with one,*
*they never reach a known limit.*

*Since nonbeing was in its own essence pure,*
*from it appeared the 'Hidden Treasure.'*

[ 47 ]

Read the sentence, "I was a Hidden Treasure"
and become aware of the elusive secret.

Nonbeing is a mirror, the world its reflection, and man
is the eye of this reflection, beholding the hidden Viewer.

140    You are the reflection's eye and It the light of the eye.
The Light of the eye is seeing itself through your eye!

The universe is human, and the human a universe.
It cannot be made any clearer than this!

When you look well into the heart of this matter,
God is the seer, the seen, and sight itself.

A sacred Tradition has explained this meaning:
"I am his hearing and his seeing," makes it clear.

Know that the world from end to end is a mirror.
In each atom blaze one hundred shining suns.

145    If you cleave the heart of a drop of water,
a hundred pure oceans will flow from it.

Each speck of dust, carefully examined,
reveals thousands of humans teeming within.

A gnat's legs are like those of an elephant.
A drop of water suggests the great River Nile.

[ 48 ]

From the core of a seed spring a hundred harvests.
A whole world comes out of a seed of grass.

Spirit dwells in a mosquito's wing.
Heaven's sphere is in the point of its eye.

In the niche known as the core of the heart,                    150
the Lord of the Two Worlds makes a home.

Within the heart both worlds have been joined,
sometimes showing Satan, and sometimes Adam.

Look at the world where everything is topsy-turvy:
Within an angel lies a demon, in the devil is an angel.

All are mingled together like a seed and its fruit.
In the denier see a believer, in a believer see denial.

All have been assembled in the point of the moment;
All cycles of time itself: the days, months, and years.

Pre-creation and eternity are here merged together:           155
the final coming of Jesus and the making of Adam.

At every point linked along this great cycle,
thousands of forms emerge and take on shape.

A circle appears around each of these points
which are centers orbiting along the greater cycle.

If but one particle is pulled from its allotted place,
the whole created world would fall into chaos.

All are in a dizzy whirl and not one of these particles
has set foot outside of the limits of contingency.

160    Individual determination has imprisoned every one,
out of the Whole and into hopeless fragmentation.

You could say that they are between motion and restraint,
forever between the vestment and divestment [of Being].

All are agitating while yet ever at rest;
nor are their origins and terminations obvious.

All are yet aware of their own essence
and so make their way to that Court.

Hiding behind the veil of each and every atom
is the enlivening beauty of the Beloved's face.

 FORMULATION

165    You have heard mere words about this world.
Come tell me now, what have you seen of it?

What have you understood about form versus meaning?
What is the Other World and what is this world?

Tell me what are the Simurgh, and Qaf mountain?
What are Heaven, Hell, and the heights of Purgatory?

Which then is the Unseen World
whose day is equal to one of our years?

The Other World is not this one that you see.
Haven't you heard the verse, "And what you don't see?"

Come, tell what is [the mythical place] Jabulqa? 170
Which world is meant by the "City of Jabulsa"?

Consider what is meant by "Easts and Wests"
since there is but one of each in this world.

Hear of Ibn Abbas' allusion to "Resembling them,"
then proceed to the knowing of your own self.

You are sound asleep and your 'sight' is but a dream.
Everything that you see is merely a similitude [of Reality].

At Resurrection's dawn when you finally awake,
you'll understand that this was all illusion.

When double-vision's illusion lifts away, 175
the earth and heavens will be transfigured.

When the true Sun shows you clearly its face,
the lights of Venus, the moon, and sun won't remain.

Should a ray from that Sun strike a granite mass,
it would be blown to shreds like strands of wool.

Know that you should act now while you're able.
When you're unable, of what value your knowledge?

What words from the world of the heart shall I speak,
O crestfallen one with your feet deep in the mud?

180    The world was created for you, but you seem powerless.
Has anyone so pitiful as you ever been seen?

You are like the prisoners sitting in a cell,
whose feeble hands have shackled their own feet.

You sit like women in a corner of misfortune,
unwilling to modify the ignorance that fills you.

The brave warriors of this world are stained in blood
while you remain in hiding, unable to set foot outside.

What have you understood of the faith of the humble
that you should allow yourself such ignorance?

185    Though women are deficient in faith and understanding,
why should men choose to follow in their path?

If you are a man, come out and look [for the Real].
Pass by anything that comes to distract you.

Do not pause day or night at any of the stages.
Don't be delayed by fellow travelers or the caravan.

Go seek Truth like Abraham, the "friend of God."
Turn night to day and day to night [in ceaseless striving].

Stars and moon and the brightly shining sun
represent the senses, imagination, and brilliant intellect.

Turn away from all of these, O traveler, and keep going.     190
Just keep saying, "I love not they that set."

And like Moses, Imran's son, follow this path.
Strive until you hear, "Truly, I am God."

While still facing your mountain of unreal existence,
your cry, "Show me!" encounters, "You can't see Me."

True Reality is amber pulling at your essence of straw.
If not for your self's mountain, what distance the path?

If theophany were to strike this mountain of 'existence,'
it would be abased like the dust of the road.

A beggar is a king from one 'divine attraction.'     195
In an instant a mountain is a mound of straw.

Follow Master Muhammad's path in his ascension.
Go explore and observe all of the mighty signs.

Come out from the courtyard of Umm Hani.
Say with certainty, "Who sees me [has seen the Real]."

Transcend the universe's constricted corner.
Remain in the "closeness of two bows' lengths."

God will then give you anything you desire.
He will show you "things as they really are."

### ANOTHER FORMULATION

200    For the soul that experiences God's revelation,
all the world is like Truth's book, Most High.

'Accidents' are like its vowels and 'substance' its consonants,
the varied levels of creatures like its verses and pauses.

Each of the worlds is like a specific Koranic chapter.
One is the Fātiḥa and another, the Ikhlāṣ.

The very first verse was the Universal Intellect.
As such it resembles the B of Bismillāh.

Second came the Universal Soul like the Verse of Light
which was like a lamp of exceedingly brilliant light.

205    The third verse to appear was the Throne of the Merciful.
Know that the fourth verse was that of His Footstool.

After this came words concerning the [seven] heavens.
In them are found the Sura of the Seven Verses.

Now look at the bodies made of the elements.
Each one of them is a manifest sign.

After these come mineral, vegetable, and animal bodies
for which it's impossible to count all the signs.

The last to descend [to this realm] is the human soul,
for which reason the Koran ends with the chapter "Man."

### CONTEMPLATION IN
### THE HORIZONS

Don't be a prisoner of the elements and their natures.          210
Come out and gaze upon God's works.

Meditate on the creation of the vast heavens,
that you may praise the Real for these signs.

See how the great sphere of the Throne
completely surrounds the two worlds.

Why was it named the Throne of the Merciful?
What relation has it to the human heart?

Why are these two forever in motion,
and not for a moment coming to rest?

215 Is not the center of heaven's Throne the heart,
like a point 'round which the great sphere turns?

In the span of a night and day, more or less,
the Throne circles around you, O dervish!

It moves the heavenly bodies in circling motion.
But why such motion? Take a careful look at this.

From East to West just like a water-wheel,
they're always moving free from food and sleep.

For every day and night, the spherical Throne
makes a complete rotation around this world.

220 And from its motion turn the other heavens.
They are spheres within, also in rotation.

But, contrary to the Great Sphere's rotation,
these eight spheres spin in the other direction.

The Ecliptic is the adjuster of the zodiac,
since it has neither change nor discrepancy.

Aries, Taurus, Gemini and Cancer, along with
Leo and Virgo are suspended from it.

Libra and Scorpio along with Sagittarius
are seen there with Capricorn, Aquarius and Pisces.

There are one thousand and twenty-four fixed stars          225
which have their own stations on the eighth sphere.

Saturn is the keeper of the seventh sphere.
The sixth sphere is the home of Jupiter.

The fifth heaven is the place of Mars.
In the fourth is our sun which adorns the world.

Third is that of Venus and second is the place of Mercury.
The moon travels in the sphere of our own earth.

Saturn in the house of Capricorn and Aquarius, and
Jupiter in Sagittarius and Pisces, increase and decrease.

Mars is placed in the house of Aries and Scorpio.          230
The sun comes to rest in the house of Leo.

Venus has made its corner in Taurus and Libra
while Mercury has gone into Gemini and Virgo.

The moon sees in Cancer one similar to herself.
When her 'tail' becomes her 'head' it makes a knot.

The moon passes through twenty-eight houses,
then becomes [full and] opposite the sun.

[ 57 ]

Later she becomes [thin] like an old palm frond
as determined by the Powerful, the Knowing One.

235 If you reflect upon this, O Perfect Man,
you would say that it was not made in vain.

The words of God's scripture are clear about this.
Thinking creation's in vain is "the view of unbelievers."

The existence of a mosquito is proof of great wisdom.
Is it not then found in Mercury or Mars?

Yet when considering the heart of this matter,
see the firmament subject to the Powerful's will.

Since the astrologer has no share of true faith,
he claims that earthly effects originate in the sky.

240 He does not see that the revolving spheres
are really under the Real's command.

 ILLUSTRATION

You could say that these revolving heavens
turn day and night like a potter's wheel.

Ever turning through the wisdom of its master
and forming another vessel of water and clay.

All that is within time and within space,
is of but one master and one workshop.

If the planets were really all such perfect ones,
why are they each at times in retrograde?

Why are their orbits, colors, and shapes,                    245
subject to such different states?

Why sometimes in perigee and then in apogee,
sometimes solitary and then in conjunction?

What makes the inner firmament full of fire,
and with a desire for Whom does it agitate?

All the stars started turning because of Him,
sometimes high above and sometimes below [our earth].

The elements of water, air, fire, and earth
have found their places beneath the firmament.

Each acts in its own center of influence,                    250
unable to step this way or that by an atom's span.

The four of them are opposed in nature and scope,
yet has anyone seen how they join [as creation]?

Each of them is opposed in essence and appearance,
yet they will combine by virtue of necessity.

The three realms of nature have arisen from them:
Mineral, plant, and animal existences.

Primal matter is then put by the elements in between.
Sufi-like, they are abstracted from individual form.

255    All through God's command and wisdom
stand in place, subject to His Will.

The mineral world clings to earth through His might.
The plant realm stands erect by His love.

The passion of animals is made of His sincerity,
each striving to preserve genera and individuals of species.

All recognize the authority of their master.
All [inwardly] strive for Him day and night.

CONTEMPLATION
WITHIN SOULS

Take a close look at your own true origins:
The [earthly] mother had a father who was also a mother.

260    Behold in yourself the world from end to end.
See all that exists as pre-existing within.

Though Adam's form was last to appear,
both worlds are dependent on his essence.

Is not the last the reason for creation after all?
Didn't Adam come into being from his own essence?

Dark-heartedness and ignorance are opposite to light
yet they are where the divine manifestations occur.

Because the back of a mirror is dense and dark,
on its front face it will show a person's face.

The rays of the sun shining from the fourth sphere          265
cannot be reflected except on dense earth.

You're the reflection of That worshiped by the angels,
who for that reason prostrate before you.

Every creature's body has a spirit related to yours
and a cord that is tied to you from each of them.

The reason [creatures] are subject to your command
is that the spirit of each of them is found in you.

You are the kernel of this world and are at its center.
Know yourself! You are the very spirit of this world.

The temperate northern latitudes became your home          270
like your heart taking shelter in your left side.

The worlds of mind and spirit are your resources.
The earth and the sky are there to adorn you.

Consider the nonbeing that is the very Being!
Observe sublimity in the essence of baseness.

Your natural powers are ten thousand in number.
Your impulses are beyond limit and counting.

This [complexity] is dependent upon instruments
such as your limbs, muscles, and members.

275 Physicians are completely confounded because of them.
They find themselves at a loss to explain such anatomy.

Not one of them has taken up this task [of understanding]
without confessing that it was beyond his power.

Each of the organs receives its portion from the Real.
The origin and dissolution of each come through a Name.

All beings have secured existence through a Name.
By that Name they perpetually worship the Real.

In origin, each being arises from that source.
On returning, that Name is like a door.

280 By the door through which it arrived it will return,
even if it passes from door to door in this life.

That is how you've known all of the Names,
since you are the reflected form of the Named.

The manifestations of Power, Knowledge, and Will
are in you, O servant of the Lord of Felicity!

You are hearing, seeing, living, and speaking.
You subsist from There and not from yourself.

O First who are in essence the Last!
O Hidden who are in essence the Apparent!

All day and night you worry about yourself.                    285
Better that you didn't know about yourself.

Reflection leads to bewilderment in the end
so here ends further debate on reflection.

❖ ❖ ❖

The first two inquiries concerned themselves with thought and reflection. In the third inquiry, Sayyid Husseini asks what self is. What is the 'I' which people have identified with? How does one get to know its source? Shabistari answers that the true identity of a person is an aspect of the Divine. He writes:

> When Absolute Existence is alluded to,
> People use the word 'I' as a matter of expression.

In his *Mafātīḥ al-iʿjāz fī sharḥ Gulshan-i rāz* (Keys to the Wondrous Eloquence in the Exegesis of the *Gulshan-i rāz*) Muhammad Lahiji writes:

> When Absolute Reality, which is absolute existence, limits Itself, It leaves the Absolute, invisible world to penetrate the visible one. You then name It 'I.' In effect, 'I' is nothing more than this Absolute Reality which has limited Itself, and all the pronouns, 'me,' 'you,' 'him,' only designate It. There is no possibility of duality in the Divine Unity.

Lahiji does not mean that the personality with which most people identify is Divine. He means that if one penetrates to what is beyond the delimitation of this personality, one finds only the Divine remaining. Here is his summary of this process:

[ 64 ]

*It is necessary to make a spiritual journey outside of spatial dimension and corporeal existence; leaving the world of Names and Attributes. You then transcend the plane of multiplicity and individuality; and attain the plane of the Absolute through annihilation of corporeal and spiritual existence. In this way you reach permanent existence in God. At that point, you will be able to see that the entire creation and all things in it are parts of yourself, that you penetrate every molecule of everything, and that there is nothing outside of 'you.' Thus you understand that there exists nothing outside of your 'I.'*

Human consciousness is the interface between pure Being and the illusion of separate identity. It is the meeting place of the Divine and Its own delimitation, which has relative existence consisting in the particularizations of this world. Shabistari likens this situation to an Arabic letter which resembles a face, on which the two eyes represent respectively the Divine 'I' and the phenomenal 'I.' When the phenomenal 'I' is transcended through Sufi exercises, the 'I' of the Real is left. So we must be careful here not to infer that the phenomenal identity actually merges with the Real or that in some way it becomes the Real. In many other places in the *Garden of Mystery,* Shabistari clearly states that this is not the case.

*Who am I? Explain to me who I am.*
*What does it mean to "make the journey within oneself"?*

❧ REPLY ❧

*Now you ask me, "what is 'me'?"*
*You ask for an explanation of "who am I?"*

*When Absolute Existence is alluded to,*
*people use the word 'I' as a matter of expression.*

290     *When Reality has taken form through individuation,*
*you refer to It in language with the word 'I.'*

*You and I are 'accidents' of the Essence of Being,*
*like openings in the covering of the lamp of Being.*

*Know all light as the same, whether of spirits or bodies,*
*sometimes shining from the mirror, sometimes the lamp.*

*You say that the word 'I' used in expressions*
*is meant to indicate its source in spirit.*

*But since you've adopted reason as your guide*
*you do not know 'yourself' from your separate parts.*

Go my friend and understand yourself well
but don't mistake swelling for the fullness of health.

This 'I' of yours is actually above body and soul
since these two are of the parts of this 'I.'

The word 'I' does not exclusively refer to humankind
that you could say it refers solely to the human spirit.

Travel the path that leads beyond this universe.
Leave this world and hide your self within the Self.

From an imaginary script writing the word identity,
two i's will appear at the moment of vision.

Nothing is left of the seeker, nor of the path,
when these i's are absorbed in the I of Reality.

Being is Heaven and phenomena are a Hell.
Your 'I' in between is the barzakh, the interface.

When this veil [of identity] is lifted from before you,
the laws of religion and its sects disappear.

All the religious rules are because of your 'I'
since the latter is tied to the human body and spirit.

When this 'I' of yours is no longer remaining,
what place have the Kaʿba, synagogue or monastery?

[ 67 ]

305  This separate I is like a speck in your eye.
     When your eye is cleared, forms reveal the Essence.

     The path of the seeker is not more than two steps,
     although it does have a number of risks.

     The first is to transcend the outer forms of Identity.
     The second is to traverse this desert of existence.

     The One here is witnessed as ones and their sum,
     just as the essence of numbers is 'one.'

     You're the comprehensiveness that is Unity itself.
     You are the Unity that has become multiplicity.

310  The person who knows this road has abandoned self
     and from partiality made the journey to the Whole.

Having established in the third inquiry that the real nature
of personal existence is illusion, and that the only real being
is with God, Shabistari answers questions about the seeker
of spiritual truth and the Completed Person accordingly.
This process is described as a purification from worldliness
and from the limitations that caused separate consciousness
to arise in the first place. Shabistari's explanation of human
development starts with a description of the human synthesis of matter and Spirit. Such a synthesis leads to a sensory
apprehension of the world and the appearance of feelings,
such as desire and anger, which are the root of separation
from the infinite Spirit in each person. The person either
realizes this and turns to his or her origin or remains trapped
in the veils of multiplicity. If he or she turns toward Spirit,
then an inner unfolding, a process with known stages, begins.

Shabistari explains that there are two ways in which a
person may find his origin. One is *jadhbah*, the attraction
God exerts on whomever He wishes. The other is the reflection of reason, in which the mind considers all of the
signs of God around him and the words of prophets and
sages and comes to the inner realization of his own origin.
He next describes the stages and characteristics of spiritual
travel using various prophets as exemplars of each stage. In
answering the second question of this inquiry regarding
who is the completed person, Shabistari writes:

*He is a Completed Man who from his perfection*
*does the work of a servant despite his lordship.*

. . .

*He finds subsistence in God after annihilation of self.*
*From the end of his quest he returns to the beginning.*

Shabistari then takes a look at the religious Law and the arrival of prophets in their role of calling people back to the Real. He clarifies a controversy surrounding the Sufis, which involves a claim made by Ibn al-ʿArabi that sainthood has precedence over prophecy. What Ibn al-ʿArabi meant was that the nature of prophecy is based on the inner sainthood or holiness of a prophet and that the prophetic message was dependent on this closeness to God. In Islam, the Seal of the Prophets is Muhammad, and it is held that there are to be no new prophetic revelations after his time. But the line of sainthood continues all the way to the end of the world, and the invisible archetype for sainthood is the 'Seal of the Saints.' According to Lahiji, this blessed individual is to be born in a golden age near the end of the world from the family of Muhammad. He is generally known in the Islamic world as the Mahdi.

For Shabistari, each prophet represents a particular perfection of virtue, and Muhammad is the comprehensive manifestation of these perfections. Saints vary in both the degree and comprehensiveness of these perfections that correspond to attributes of earlier prophets.

*What is the traveler like, who is the wayfarer?*
*Whom can we call a Completed Man?*

∾ REPLY ∾

*Now you ask me who is the traveler on the Way.*
*It's whoever's become aware of the Origin.*

*The wayfarer is one who passes along swiftly,*
*becoming purified from self like fire from smoke.*

*Know his journey as revelatory travel from contingency*
*toward the Necessary by abandoning faults and deficiency.*

*Reversing the first journey to this realm, stage by stage,*          315
*the traveler goes on to become the Completed Person.*

∾ FORMULATION ∾

*First know in what manner the human's coming into being*
*leads to aim of manifesting the Completed Person.*

*He appeared in the realms of inanimate matter.*
*With the expansion of Spirit he became aware.*

He then stirred through God's Power
and came to have his will through the Real.

Worldly sensations opened in his childhood
which is just what led to Adam's temptation.

320  As earthly particulars became arranged in his mind,
he came to understand the whole by combining them.

Anger and lust then manifested in him
and with them possessiveness, greed, and pride.

All sorts of blameworthy qualities struggled in him
making him worse than a wild animal, devil or demon.

This is the lowest point in Being's descent
because it is the point opposite to Unity.

Actions give rise to endless multiplicity
and so he became inverted to his Origin.

325  If he remains bound by the fetters of this snare
he will become less than cattle in misguidedness.

And if a light shines on him from the spiritual world,
whether the blessing of attraction or reflection of reason,

his heart becomes intimate with the Love of the Real,
and he returns [to the Real] by the way he came.

Whether by mystical attraction or the proof of certainty,
he finds the way to the Faith of Certainty.

He rises out of hell's lowest dungeon
and turns his face toward the highest heaven.

In that moment he is truly repentant,                          330
becoming one of Adam's chosen sons.

When purified of blameworthy actions,
he rises into the heavens like Idris.

Finding deliverance from unworthy qualities
he becomes like Noah, a master of constancy.

His partial powers vanish in the Universal Will.
He'll then be like Abraham, the possessor of trust.

With his own will tied to satisfaction in God
like Moses he enters through the highest gate.

Abandoning his own limited knowledge                           335
he becomes like Jesus, of celestial nature.

He surrenders his existence to God's plundering
and follows Muhammad on his miraculous ascension.

When the farthest point has rejoined the original First,
there is no room there for angel nor prophet.

The prophet is like the sun, the saint like the moon,
facing each other in "I have a time with God."

In its innate perfection prophecy is completely pure.
Sanctity is openly shown in prophecy, not concealed.

340  The sanctity of a saint must necessarily be concealed
but with the prophet it is to be manifested openly.

By following the prophet the saint finds fellowship,
becoming an intimate of the prophet in sainthood.

The verse, "If you love Allah, follow me," guides
to the inner sanctuary of, "Allah will love you."

In that inner sanctuary he is loved by God.
Through God he becomes divinely attracted.

He is a follower but through spiritual insight.
He is a worshiper but in the alley-way of Spirit.

345  The work of the saint is finally completed
when it returns to the very beginning.

He is a Completed Man who from his perfection
does the work of a servant despite his lordship.

When he has cut across the distance [of separation],
God sets a crown on his head as Earth's vicegerent.

He finds subsistence in God after annihilation of self.
From the end of his quest he returns to the beginning.

He makes the religious Law his garment,
and the mystic path his cloak [of exaltation].

Know that the Reality is the station of his essence.                    350
His comprehensiveness spans True Faith and unbelief.

He is now endowed with praiseworthy virtues.
He is known for his knowledge, abstinence, and piety.

All the virtues are his but he is far from all,
sheltered under the [inner] domes of spiritual mystery.

The almond kernel will be completely ruined
if removed from its shell before ripening.

It is good when ripened and taken from its shell.
You must split the shell to get to the kernel.

355  Religious Law is the shell and the Reality the kernel.
Between these two lies the Sufi way.

Harm on the path occurs when the kernel is flawed.
When truly ripe, the shelled kernel is excellent.

When [one sort of] gnostic is merged in inner certainty,
the kernel ripens and breaks through the shell.

Nothing abides of his being in this world.
He leaves it to never again return.

And if the sun [of guidance] shines on the shell,
a seedling emerges to make yet another round.

360  It grows into a blessed tree nourished by water and earth.
Its branches reach up into the Seventh Heaven.

When the same [divine] seed sprouts up again,
one becomes one hundred by decree of the Powerful.

Just as a seed grows into the line of a tree,
from the point a line is drawn making another circle.

When the traveler finds completion within this circle,
the last point [of Unity] is joined to the first point.

Again like the line of a compass,
this circular progression repeats itself.

This is not about transmigration but really concerns          365
God's manifestations occurring through theophany.

They ask: "What is the ultimate spiritual goal?"
The reply is: "A return to the journey's beginning."


      ◦ FORMULATION ◦

The appearance of prophecy was with Adam.
Its completion was in Muhammad, prophecy's seal.

Sainthood remained to make a journey of its own
like a point making its own circling of the world.

Its full manifestation will come with the Seal of the Saints.
With him the circling of this world will be completed.

Individual saints exist as limbs of this Seal          370
since he is the whole for whom they are parts.

[ 77 ]

He will be related by family and name to Muhammad.
Universal Mercy will be manifested through him.

He shall be the leader of both of the worlds.
He shall be God's vicegerent for Adam's race.

The light of the sun was made separate from the night,
so you came to know of its dawn, rise, and zenith.

As heaven's wheel circles around again,
evening and dusk are revealed in the setting sun.

375    The light of the Prophet is the supreme sun,
here shining from Moses and there from Adam.

If you study the history of the world,
you will know the degree reached by each prophet.

Every moment another shadow was cast by the sun
which was another rung for the ascension of Faith.

The age of Master Muhammad was the sun's zenith,
purified of any shadow or darkness.

He was upright under the meridian of the sun
casting no shadow in front or back, left or right.

When he was stationed on God's straight path,                    380
from the command "Be steadfast," he found his stature.

He cast no shadow since that would cause darkness.
What glorious divine light, O luminous shadow of God!

His qiblah is found between East and West
and so he is fully drowned there in light.

By his hand [the inner] Satan became a Muslim
and that shadow was concealed under his feet.

The degree of all are under his firm rank.
Terrestrial beings exist from his shadow.

By his light, sainthood spreads its shadow.                       385
Prophecy's East corresponds to sainthood's West.

For any shadow that first manifested [in prophecy],
another from [sainthood] is cast opposite to it.

Any spiritual authority who is alive at present
corresponds to one of the earlier prophets.

Since prophets partake of prophecy's full perfection
they are no doubt superior to any of the saints.

Sainthood will fully appear in the Seal of the Saints.
To the first point joins the last in the Seal.

390    Through him the world will fill with peace and faith
and the mineral and animal worlds will find life.

There will not remain in the world one impious soul.
True justice will come into complete manifestation.

Through the secret of Unity he is aware of the Truth.
In him will be shown the face of the Absolute.

This inquiry continues Shabistari's discussion of the purifications needed to clear the seeker of self in order to reveal the inner Spirit. His answer, together with Lahiji's commentary on it, allows us to compare the religious approach with the mystical. Shabistari refers to an important extra-Koranic revelation [*ḥadīth qudsī*] in which Allah reveals,

> *My servant ceases not to draw closer to Me through his intense devotion* [nawāfil] *until I love him; and when I love him, I am his ear through which he hears by Me, and his eye through which he sees by Me, and his tongue with which he speaks by Me, and his hand with which he takes by Me.*[1]

This *ḥadīth* indicates the importance of sincerity and the unremitting concentration upon God in allowing the seeker to make spiritual progress. Through such complete concentration, the practitioner becomes purified of self. Shabistari writes of four successive purifications that lead to this state: of the body, of violations of religious law, of bad habits and finally (and most importantly), of the awareness of anything other than God. Lahiji comments that the first two purifications are normal to the religious Muslim. They form the basis upon which to develop the next two purifications, which transform the consciousness of the practitioner.

---

1 Trans. R.A. Nicholson.

❀ ❀ ❀

*Who is stationed in the awareness of Unity?*
*What is known by the ʿĀrif, the Sufi gnostic?*

∽ REPLY ∽

*A person attains to the awareness of Unity*
*who doesn't stop at any spiritual station of the Way.*

395     *The heart of the ʿĀrif is the knower of Being.*
*Absolute Being is what he witnesses.*

*He knows no existence except real Existence.*
*He has lost any existence except for the Real.*

*Your existence is all thorns and weeds.*
*Make a clean sweep and throw those out.*

*Go sweep out the house of self.*
*Make ready a place for the Beloved.*

*When 'you' have left, He will come within and*
*through you, but without 'you,' display His beauty.*

Whoever is loved by God because of excessive devotion,     400
has swept out his house through self-effacement.

He is stationed in the most blessed place.
By "[God is] his hearing and seeing," found His trace.

Yet as long as the stain of personal existence remains,
the ʿĀrif's knowledge cannot penetrate to the source.

Until you have put the obstacles apart from you,
the Light will not shine in the home of your heart.

Because there are four obstacles of this world,
there are also four purifications for them.

First is the purification of the external form.     405
Second is clearing sin and the "whisperer's evil."

Third is cleaning away blameworthy habits
that keep a human being at the level of beasts.

Fourth purifies the inner consciousness of otherness
and this brings one to the end of the journey.

Whoever has completed these purifications
is doubtless prepared to speak with God.

Until you've lost every trace of 'self,'
how can your prayer be real prayer?

410   When your essence is purified of all stain of self,
      your prayer then becomes "a light for the eyes."

      There then remains no distinction in between.
      Known and knower become fully one thing.

At the end of the last inquiry, Shabistari writes:

> *There then remains no distinction in between;*
> *Known and knower become fully one thing.*

Once the individual loses his individuality and his self-identity, which are the sum of the worldly manifestations of his essential predisposition acted upon by the Divine Names, there remains only the Real. One can say that God then knows God. In this sixth inquiry, Shaikh Husseini poses the rhetorical question:

> *If the Known and the knower are both pure Essence*
> *What is the agitation of this handful of dust?*

In *The Keys to the Wondrous Eloquence in the Exegesis of the Garden of Mystery,* Lahiji writes that one should not be ungrateful because human existence is the form through which the delimited and fictitious 'existence' of this dimension manifests wisdom and a return to God. He writes that human and other creatures actually have no existence in this dimension. As immutable entities [*a'yān thābita*], they have a quasi-existence as known entities within the knowledge of the Real, but they are powerless. Through the agency of the Names, the Real manifests the potentials of the immutable entities and causes them to 'exist' in this dimension. Shabistari compares the immutable entities to

۰
۱
۲
۳
۴
۵
۶
۷
۸
۹
۱۰
۱۱
۱۲
۱۳
۱۴
۱۵

dust that is warmed and illuminated by the sun. The dust is nothing in itself but can accept the light and heat of the sun.

The immutable entities do have a pre-creational recognition of their Origin, however, and when God asks them before their manifestation in physical form, "Am I not your Lord?," they reply, "Yes!" They also have varied gnostic predispositions, some with a capacity to reflect, and therefore know, the Real, and some with little or no such capacity. The latter individuals manifest the Actions of the Real in this material dimension but remain heedless of God all of their terrestrial lives.

For those whose predispositions are such that they may know God, there is the possibility of purification and transcendence from this dimension, at which point such seekers can know what they knew before the Creation. Shabistari compares those without the predisposition for mystical experience to those who are born blind. No matter how much one tries to explain colors to them, it is not possible for them to understand. Such people may use their intellects to reject and deride the mystical quest. It is at the interface of spirit and body, which is the mystic's heart, that the fire of the original love for God can be set ablaze. Shabistari writes that spirit and body are like flint and steel. When they "strike together" through transcendence of the world of forms and devotion to God, the fire of love ignites.

If Known and knower are both pure Essence,
what is the agitation of this handful of dust?

❧ REPLY ❧

Don't be ungrateful for the blessings of God
since you may know God by His light.

There's no knower or known except the Real,
yet dust finds itself heated by the sun.

Isn't it a wonder that bits of dust have hope                    415
and desire the sun's light and warmth?

Recall the state and condition of your original nature
and regain the source of God-contemplation.

Why did God say, "Am I not your Lord?"?
Who answered in that moment, "Yes!"?

On that day when Man's clay was mixed,
the lesson of faith was written within his heart.

If you would read that script just once,
you'd know everything that you desire.

420    Only yesternight you bound yourself to service,
a promise you're unaware of through forgetfulness.

Sacred scriptures have been revealed
so that you might remember your promise.

If you've seen the Real in your original state,
you should be able to see Him in "That Place."

Look at God's Attributes 'here' today,
so you may know of His Essence tomorrow.

If you can't, don't damage yourself with sorrow.
Hear from the Koran, "You cannot guide."

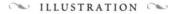 ILLUSTRATION

425    A blind man won't believe what you say about color
even if you spend a hundred years trying to prove it.

White, yellow, red, green and golden straw
will be nothing but black in front of this man.

Consider the sad state of the one born blind.
Will the oculist's eye-black bring him remedy?

Reason trying to grasp the states of the other world
is like the one born blind trying to see in this world.

However, humankind possesses a special faculty,
that he or she may come to know hidden secrets.

Like the potential for fire existing in flint and steel,       430
God has placed this faculty in spirit and body.

When these two strike together like flint and steel,
the light created illuminates the two worlds.

From that joining the mystery is revealed.
Since you've been informed, go reduce your 'self.'

Your real 'you' is a copy of the divine design.
Seek from this self anything you may desire.

*

١

٢

٣

۴

۵

۶

Mansur al-Hallaj, perhaps the most famous and controversial Sufi ever to have lived, was executed in 922 AD for allegedly uttering the blasphemy, "I am the Real [*ana al-ḥaqq*]." Innumerable stories and commentaries concerning al-Hallaj have been written in the Islamic world, ranging from calumny by the conventionally religious, to the deep reverence usually shown him by Sufis. Shabistari defends him and explains what this great mystic meant by the statement that led to his death. This defense can be summed up by the line:

> *Except for the Real, who may say, "I am the Real"?*

٧

٨

٩

١٠

١١

١٢

١٣

١۴

In the third inquiry, Shabistari explains that God is the reality within all creatures whose superficial identity results from the 'accident' of their fixed entities [*aʿyān thābita*]. If this accidental aspect of a creature is spiritually overwhelmed, what remains is God. If the creature is a Completed Human, such as was Mansur al-Hallaj, the speech that remains after self-annihilation is the speech of God. The dogmatic Muslims could not possibly understand this and thought that Mansur was claiming for himself divine incarnation. Shabistari clarifies this:

> *It's the individual formation that separates from Being.*
> *God's not become his creature nor creature joined with God.*

١۵

He then compares the apparent reality of creation to an image in a mirror. The metaphor of the reflected image is frequently used by Sufis to describe the illusion that is our world. Every creature's immutable essence is a mirror for the Divine Names to act upon and create an existence that is relative and illusory. The Completed Human is the most perfect mirror, capable of reflecting all of the Divine Names.

To what point [or level] belongs the saying, "Ana al-ḥaqq"?
What do you say? Is this ultimate riddle just nonsense?

∾ REPLY ∾

435    "Ana al-ḥaqq" is a complete unveiling of secrets.
       Except for the Real, who may say, "I am the Real"?

All of the atoms of the world just like Mansur,
you should take as ecstatic and drunk:

They're ever glorifying and exalting God
subsisting in the true meaning of ["I am the Real."]

If you want this to become easy for you,
recite the verse, "Everything is praising God."

Once you have carded the cotton of 'yourself,'
you too like Hallaj will breathe such words.

440    Pluck from your ears the cotton of illusion.
       Listen to the call of the One, the All-Powerful.

The call is coming from the Real without pause.
Why do you wait for the Day of Resurrection?

Come into the Valley of Aiman where unawares,
you'll hear the burning bush say, "Truly, I am God."

Anyone with no trace of doubt in his heart
knows with certainty of no existence except One.

"I am the Real" is fitting speech for God,
since 'He' implies an absence and that is illusion.

The Exalted Presence of the Real has no duality.                    445
In that Presence there is no me, you, or we.

Me, you, and we are but one and the same thing
since in the Unity there is no distinguishing.

Anyone who has been emptied like a void
will echo, "I am the Real" from deep within.

His lordly aspect subsists while 'otherness' perishes.
Traveling, the road, and the traveler become One.

Thoughts here of incarnation or union are impossible
since within Unity such duality is the essence of error.

Ideas of incarnation and union arise from 'otherness'           450
but Unity emerges from spiritual progression.

It's the individual formation that separates from Being.
God's not become his creature nor creature joined with God.

Creation's being and multiplicity are an appearance.
Not all of that which appears is of real Being.

## ILLUSTRATIONS OF APPEARANCES
## WITHOUT REALITY

Place a mirror in front of yourself;
Look and see the other person in it.

Look at it carefully and ask, "Who is that image?"
It is neither self nor mirror, so what is this image?

455   Since I am fixed in my essential self,
I do not know what is this shadow-me.

How can nonbeing be joined to Existence?
Light and darkness cannot really be conjoined.

Like time past, future months and years are naught.
What is there really but this one point of the moment?

It is one imaginary point that has been in motion.
You have [erroneously] named it a flowing stream.

Except for Me, who else is to be found in this desert?
Tell me, what are these sounds and echoes around Me?

"Accidents are transient, substance compounded of them."     460
Tell, what is substance or where is it really compounded?

Bodies emerge with length, breadth, and depth,
but can what exists arise from such nothingness?

The whole world has this nature as its basis.
Since you now know, be firm in the Faith.

Except for the Real there's no other existence.
So say, "He is the Real," or, "I am the Real" as you wish.

Separate illusory manifestations from real Existence.
Don't be a stranger, get to know your [real] Self.

This inquiry concerns itself with the metaphysics of non-being and the metaphysical exigency for the illusory entity we know as the 'self.' We could summarize by saying that the self exists in order to fulfill the intention found in the words of God: "I was a hidden treasure and I longed to be known. I created man and the cosmos so that I would be known." Ibn al-'Arabi has written that God's knowing Himself in Himself is different from knowing Himself through the mirror of the completed person. Adam was the first completed person, representing the reflective capacity of the world of forms. Yet the self in its ordinary human condition of being veiled from Reality is like the dust and impurity that corrupts that Adamic mirror. This corrupting of human consciousness is described in the Koran: "Their hearts are tarnished by what they have acquired." In other words, this loss of reflectivity occurs through an attachment to the world of forms. As this tarnish is scoured from the mirror, deeper levels of the self are experienced. The Completed Person ultimately experiences that the self is only a reflection of the Real.

Shabistari explores the nature of nonbeing. According to the philosophers, this world's matter arises out of *substance* (the simple essence of anything that is not seen unless it takes on form) and *accident* (the particular form of a thing, that could not manifest except that it is grounded in its substance). These are borrowed Peripatetic definitions of matter [*hayūlā*], called *materia prima* in Western metaphysics. Shabistari claims that there is no reality to this matter or its manifestations:

> But what is matter except absolute nonbeing,
> Which takes on the forms and shapes that are known?

He goes on to describe the natural order, which intends from the beginning the human form. Nature is the outer manifestation of the Divine Imagination, in which a delimitation of Being takes place. In this process, the comprehensive mirror of the Completed Person emerges to reflect the limitless Origin. All of creation arises out of Oneness and returns to the One in this beautiful and terrifying process.

465   *Why is it said that the human creature reaches union?*
*How does his spiritual journeying reach its aim?*

*Union with the Real is separation from createdness.*
*Estrangement from oneself is acquaintance with the Real.*

*When the contingent removes the dust of contingency,*
*except for the Necessary, nothing remains.*

*The existence of the two worlds is like a fantasy.*
*In its moment of subsistence is its very perishing.*

*That which has united [with God] is not His creature.*
*Such words are not spoken by the Completed Person.*

470   *When has nonbeing ever entered through this door?*
*What relation has dust to the Lord of Lords?*

*What is nonbeing that it should unite with the Real,*
*and of nonbeing make spiritual journeying and progression?*

*If your soul were aware of the real meaning of this,*
*you would in that moment exclaim, "God forgive me!"*

You are non-existent, abiding forever in nonbeing!
When can such nonbeing reach the Necessary?

Substance does not manifest without its accident.
What's the accident? What doesn't last two moments.

A *philosopher who's written about the natural order*                     475
has described things by length, width, and depth.

But what is matter but a complete nonexistent
through which the shapes and forms are actualized?

Just as originally there is no form without matter,
matter without form is also just nonbeing.

Cosmic bodies have come from these two nonexistents.
Except for their unreality, nothing else is known.

See your own nature, that is not more nor less:
Not existing, and not nonexistent in yourself.

From within Reality take a look at contingent phenomena.        480
They are without real Existence, the essence of privation.

Being in its own perfection permeates Itself.
Individual forms are just fictitious manifestations.

Truly, these fictitious manifestations are not existent.
Numbers are many but only one is being counted.

This world has no existence except in appearance.
End to end, its work is frolic and play.

From the sea a wet mist rises into the sky.
By the Real's command it rains down on the desert.

485  Sun's rays from the fourth celestial sphere
shine down and nourish a fertile mixture.

The sun's warmth rises back into the atmosphere.
Suspending the humidity of that same sea water.

When these are conjoined with earth and air,
lush greenery and trees come forth.

These become the nourishment of the animals
that in turn become the food assimilated by man.

Of food is made a sperm-drop that develops [in the womb]
growing into the form of another human being.

490  When the light of the 'rational soul' pervades the body,
a subtle, luminescent body comes into existence.

The child becomes a youth, an adult, an old man,
possessed of intellect, judgment, understanding and logic,

Until the time of death set by the Pure Presence
when pure returns to the Pure and dust to dust.

All the parts of this world are like those plants
that are really just one drop from the ocean of life.

When their time has elapsed they return to it,
their completion puts them all as they were in origin.

Each of them travels back to its center of origin,                    495
since nature never abandons the character of the center.

Unity is like an ocean but one full of blood.
Thousands of crazed waves surge from it.

Look at the drops of rain rising up from this sea.
Countless are the forms and their names:

Mist and cloud, rain and moist clay,
plant life, animals, and finally the Completed Person,

all was just a drop of water at the beginning
from which all of these things have been formed.

Know the world of Intellect, Soul, heavens, and planets             500
to be like that one drop from beginning to end.

When death strikes the heavens and stars,
all of existence will become lost in nonbeing.

When that wave strikes, the world will be obliterated,
certainly "As though it had not existed yesterday."

In an instant the fantasy will be gone,
nothing remaining except for Reality.

You reach nearness in that same moment,
without your 'you,' united with the Beloved.

505   In union, the fantasy of 'you' ends.
Only when the 'other' vanishes is there union.

Don't say the contingent has transcended its limits.
It has not become the Necessary, nor the Necessary it.

Whoever has excelled in spiritual knowledge
won't speak this inversion of the realities.

You've thousands of creations before you, sir.
Go consider your coming and going in them.

In discussing the part and the whole of human life:
One by one I'll reveal them leaving nothing obscure.

TRANSLATOR'S INTRODUCTION
TO THE NINTH INQUIRY

This inquiry concerns the apparent separation of God and
creation. Here, Mir Husseini uses terminology inherited
from Greek philosophy, that of the 'contingent' and the
'Necessary.' He also asks about the opposites of 'near' and
'far,' and 'more' and 'less.' Shabistari again returns to the
theme of real Being residing within as the essential reality
of all things. He again advises that if the seeker transcends
his limited self, he will find Being remaining.

The illusion of free will is examined in some detail. In
an exoteric study of Islam (and most other religions), the
question of free will has always been a source of confusion.
A reading of scriptural prohibitions, admonitions, and directives is usually interpreted by commentators to mean
that there must be free choice. Otherwise, why would these
prohibitions and directives exist? Mystics, on the other hand,
usually deny that there is any real freedom of choice. They
point to other verses in the various scriptures to show that
God has predetermined all things. In truth, though, it is
especially their experience of self-annihilation that informs
them about this question.

It is not surprising that mystics should hold a view of
radical determinism, since they describe their mystical experience, in part, as the experience of only one Reality, or one
Player manifesting within the vast multiplicity of created
forms. We could summarize their position by saying that
there is really only one Being and one event occurring at

any time, even though there appears to be vast multiplicity. The multiplicity emanating from the one Being is dreamlike, only an exploration of delimitation on the part of the Unlimited. Individuals participate in the dream by fulfilling the condition of the divine modality known as 'differentiation,' wherein the Divine establishes multi-polar awareness. It is only natural that the entities should think that they have freedom of choice.

The reader may wonder how mystics explain scriptural admonitions and directives. Although the response varies from mystic to mystic, many Sufis answer that scriptural directives activate laudable predispositions existing since pre-creation in the immutable entities [al-a'yān al-thābita]. These predispositions vary a great deal and the influence of a source of spiritual teaching can activate spirituality in a person if that is his or her destiny.

The unlimited knowledge of the Real encompasses all the possibilities of the immutable entities from pre-eternity, and the Real's power predetermines the entity's actions. So to the extent that a person has the predisposition to uncover Spirit within, the Real acts upon that predisposition, which is the basis of spiritual guidance whether from scripture or from a teacher. The predisposition of the Completed Human is that he or she is the comprehensive locus for all of the Divine Names. The spiritual heart of the Completed Human is a mirror for all the Names within this illusion we call the world and is also continuous with the Divine Unity.

✿ ✿ ✿

What is the union of the contingent and the Necessary?          510
What mean the words near and far, more and less?

∾ REPLY ∾

Now listen to what I say, not more nor less.
From nearness [to illusion] you've fallen far from yourself.

Since it's really an appearance of Being within nonbeing,
that's where 'near and far,' and 'more and less' arise.

Near is that one on whom the Light is shining.
Far is that nonbeing which is far from existing.

If a Light from the Self reaches within you,
it frees you from your personal existence.

What have you achieved between Being and nonbeing?          515
You are one moment afraid and the next full of hope.

Whoever knows Him does not fear Him,
yet a child is afraid of his own shadow.

No fear will remain if you set out [on the Way].
The Arab steed needs no prodding of the whip.

What fear can you have of the fire of hell
when your body and soul are purified of existence?

When pure gold is melted in a furnace blaze,
as it has no impurity, what can burn away?

520    There is nothing in the way except your self,
but beware of the tenacious existence of the self.

If you become trapped in yourself,
the world will at once become your veil.

The basest place in the circle of existence,
you-ness is the point opposite to Unity.

The phenomena of this world have affected you,
and you say with Satan, "Who is there like me?"

Because of this you say, "I have authority and free will.
My body is a steed and my soul is its rider."

525    "The reins of the body are in the hands of the soul.
That is why religious directives are assigned me."

Don't you know that this is the way of fire-worshipers?
All this calamity and ill-luck arise from [relative] existence.

What kind of free will is this, my ignorant man,
when in his essential nature a person is nonexistent?

Since your being is truly nonbeing,
don't you wonder about your "free will?"

Since a person's existence is not of himself,
good and bad cannot be attributed to his essence.

Who have you seen in the whole of this world                    530
who's found a moment of joy without some pain?

Say who has achieved the measure of his hopes
and remained in that state of perfection?

Attainments endure yet those who attain
are under His command: "God is the Overwhelmer."

Know that the Real causes effects everywhere.
Don't set foot outside of your own limit [of nonbeing].

Ask from your own state about destiny.
Come to know [the folly of ] those spouting free will.

One whose religion denies divine determinism                    535
has been likened by the Prophet to a Zoroastrian.

Just as the Zoroastrian speaks of Yazdan and Ahriman,
that stupid fool speaks of you and we.

Attributing actions to ourselves is just imagination.
Such attribution is really jest and amusement.

You didn't exist when your actions were created.
You were chosen to accomplish a special purpose.

Through the immeasurable power of the Real,
through Knowledge, He gave the absolute command:

540   All is predestined prior to spirit and body,
the purpose of every entity is determined.

One worshipped for seven hundred thousand years,
then was made to wear the yoke of [God's] curse.

Another, after sinning, came to know Light and Purity.
After repenting he came to be known as 'chosen.'

Even stranger is that through [Satan's] disobedience
[Adam] was blessed through God's mercy and forgiveness.

Yet [Satan] through his transgression was cursed.
O wonder of Your actions above why, what, and how!

545   O Lord of Glory and Power! It is fitting that
You transcend the fancies of your creatures.

O disputer, how is it that from pre-eternity
one was to be Muhammad and another Abu Jahl?

Whoever questions God concerning why and how
speaks blasphemy to the High Presence.

It is right for God to ask about how and what.
Objections by His creature are not fitting.

All real lordship resides in Absolute Power.
Reasons and causes are not tied to God's actions.

It's fitting for God to show mercy and wrath.                    550
Proper to His servant are obligation and poverty.

[Even] man's miracles are constrained [by God],
not evincing any portion of free choice.

Nothing ever actually came from man himself
and yet he is asked to account for good and bad.

He has no free will but is given a task.
O wonder, this beggar of constrained free choice!

It's not cruelty but essential Justice and Knowledge.
This isn't oppression but true kindness and favor.

This is why God imposed the Law upon you                         555
and defined it from your essential nature.

When you're humbled from this duty to God,
you will then rise up outside of yourself.

In the Whole you find deliverance from yourself.
You'll be rich with the Real, O Dervish!

Go, soul of your father, give your being to His decree.
Be in accord with His divine predestination.

In preceding inquiries, Shabistari explains that the lifting
away of individual 'determinations' allows Being to reveal
Itself in the human consciousness. This experience not only
begins the real life of the mystic, but also results in his or
her attempts to communicate the mystical experience, or
at least indications of it. In the tenth inquiry, Shabistari
explores relationships between the outer and the inner, the
words and their inner meaning. To Mir Husseini's questions,
"What is the sea whose shore is speech? What is the Pearl to
be found in its depths?", Shabistari answers:

> *The sea is Being and speech is its shore.*
> *Shells are words, Pearls are heart-knowledge.*

He offers a symbol to explain how meaningful poetry and
literature are created by the mystic. Like other people, the
mystic is equipped with language. His or her special capacity
for using language is symbolized by an oyster, which rises to
the surface of the ocean of Existence, and opens to receive
the grace of the Divine Names. When a divine raindrop falls
into the oyster shell, it closes and sinks back to the bottom
of the sea. When the diver, mind, plunges into this sea of
Being, it extracts the pearl of mystical expression from the
shell. The pearl represents the spiritual reality of the words.
The reader of mystical writings must make a similar attempt
to reach the spiritual reality.

Like literature, humankind is also made of inner and outer, and must break through the outer husk in order to find the inner Spirit. According to Shabistari, behavior arising out of spiritual gnosis, rather than discursive knowledge, results in right action. Shabistari further explores the way to the inner Spirit which, as we have already seen, is a way of purification. Polishing the spiritual Heart and cultivating virtues are examined. Shabistari writes that the basis of the virtues lies primarily in justice (whose word root is closely related to the idea of balance and harmony), then in wisdom, sexual restraint, and courage. He advocates the cultivation of the just mean for each of these virtues. Excess or lack of any of these four virtues is error and is the cause of sin. The proper cultivation of these virtues leads to a certain balance, which results in 'spiritual unveiling' [*kashf*]. The synthesis that emerges from balance is from the joining of a purified body and 'rational soul' wherein Spirit becomes evident. Shabistari compares this balance to the balance of the earthly elements, which synthesize as earthly beauty when they are in harmony.

What is the sea whose shore is speech?
What is the pearl to be found in its depths?


❧ REPLY ❧

The sea is Being and speech is its shore.                    560
Shells are words, pearls are heart-knowledge.

Thousands of royal pearls are tossed from each wave,
revealed in texts, traditions, and prophecies.

Thousands of waves surge from It every moment
yet It is never made less by even one drop.

The existence of Knowledge comes from that deep sea.
Its pearl is nestled in a covering of sounds and words.

When inner meanings descend to this [sensible] realm,
they must reveal themselves in allegory and metaphor.


❧ ILLUSTRATION ❧

I have heard that in springtime's month of Naisan,         565
oysters swim to the surface in the Sea of Oman.

From oceanic slopes under that sea they swim,
to float at the surface with their mouths open.

A mist then rises from the sea to the sky
and rains down by the command of the Most High.

Raindrops fall into the open shells
which close their mouths tightly around them.

With full heart, they sink back into the depths.
Each raindrop, nurtured in its shell, becomes a pearl.

570 When a sea diver plunges into those depths,
he retrieves from them resplendent pearls.

Your body is like the shore, Existence like that sea.
The mist is grace, rain is the Science of the Names.

In this great ocean, mind is the diver
whose pouch holds a hundred precious pearls.

The heart is like a vessel of Knowledge.
The shell of language covers heart-knowledge.

Breath flows like flashing lightning
forming words that reach listening ears.

575 Split the shell and bring forth a royal pearl!
Throw aside the husk, take the excellent kernel!

[ 114 ]

Words have etymology, syntax, and conjugation,
which are just the outer covering of language.

Whoever spends his whole life on these,
spends his precious life in an idle pastime.

He has only held the walnut's outer husk.
Whoever breaks the skin will find the kernel.

True, without its husk, the kernel will not ripen.
Outer knowledge sweetens the knowledge of Faith.

My dear brother, listen well to my advice to you:          580
With heart and soul, strive to the knowledge of Faith.

The informed knower is elevated in the two worlds.
Even if a lesser person, he finds greatness in knowledge.

When his actions spring from spiritual states,
it's far better than what comes of discursive knowledge.

Yet the physical actions of one's water and clay
don't lead to knowledge which is the heart's work.

See the difference between body and spirit.
Consider one the West and the other the East.

From this simile, consider the states accompanying actions          585
as they relate to the knowledge of states versus words.

What inclines to the world is not real knowledge.
Such knowing is of outer form but not of inner reality.

Real knowledge never joins with worldliness.
If you seek an angel, chase from yourself the dog.

From angelic virtues arise the knowledges of Faith.
They're not found in the heart with a dog's nature.

That's what the blessed Prophet's saying means.
Listen well, since this is its real meaning.

590    And if an image be found within this 'house,'
an angel may not approach to enter it.

Go polish the tablet of your heart
so that an angel will dwell near you.

Acquire the knowledge that is your inheritance.
For the sake of future harvest, work this field.

Read the Koran's "On the horizons and within souls."
Adorn yourself with the basis of all the virtues.

 FORMULATION

The essentials of virtue are found in equity
then wisdom, temperance, and courage.

The wise one of proper speech and action 595
is the person who's acquired these four qualities.

Through wisdom, her heart and soul are aware.
She is neither too ingenious nor simply ignorant.

She has veiled her lust with restraint
yet she's far from wantonness and abstinence.

Her courage has purified meanness and pride.
Her essence is innocent of cowardice and aggression.

With equity as the garment of her essence,
she's supplanted injustice with virtue.

All of the excellent virtues are of a middle way. 600
They exist beyond excess and abatement.

This middle is known as "the straight way."
Below either side of it are the depths of Hell.

This path is as narrow as a hair or a blade's edge
whose traveller can neither turn nor stop moving.

Equity is a virtue with only one contrary.
The virtues [as a whole] have seven contraries.

Hidden within each of these seven is a secret.
From these, count the gates of Hell as seven.

605    Just as Hell was prepared for injustice,
       paradise is a place of ever-present justice.

       The reward for justice is light and sweet mercy.
       Cruelty's reward is curses and cruel darkness.

       The appearance of goodness manifests through balance:
       The body's greatest perfection is in its balance.

       When a compound comes together as one thing,
       the action and distinction of individual parts withdraw.

       This compound becomes like a subtle essence.
       There is a link between the form and its spirit.

610    It's not just a link between the compound's parts
       since Spirit is well above the qualities of physicality.

       But when water and clay become purified,
       spirit then reaches them from the Real.

       When the elemental parts come into balance,
       the world of Spirit is illuminated within.

       The rays of Spirit shining on a body in equilibrium
       are by analogy like the sun and the earth.

Although the sun dwells in the fourth celestial sphere,
its rays are the light that manages the Earth.

The natures of earthly elements are not those of the sun.     615
Stars do not have the humors of hot, cold, dry, and moist.

Yet earthly elements are hot or cold by sun's action.
They become white, red, green, rose, and yellow.

The sun's wisdom flows like the rule of a just king.
One can't say if its effects are from without or within.

When the elements came together in perfect balance,
the rational soul fell in love with their beauty.

A *spiritual marriage* was celebrated in the Faith.
The Universal Soul gave as dowry the Earth.

From these appeared pure eloquence and     620
the various sciences, language, virtues, and beauty.

Irresistible beauty, originating in the Formless World
came into this world like an inspired libertine.

She raised Her flag above the province of beauty
and confounded the causes binding our world.

Sometimes She rides the royal steed of beauty,
sometimes She wields the shining sword of language.

As a person She is called a ravishing beauty.
Within language She is known as eloquence.

625 Whether saint or king, whether dervish or prophet,
all of them are subject to Her command.

What is in the beauty of those of lovely aspect?
It's not just earthly beauty, so tell me what is it?

Except for the Real there could not be such ravishment
and God has nothing and no person as partner.

Where can lust be said to ravish hearts
when it is the Real also manifesting in the forbidden?

Know the Real is having Its effect in every place.
Don't set foot beyond your own limits.

630 See and know the Real in Its proper garment.
The Real in the forbidden is a playground for Satan.

Mir Husseini asks, "What is the part that exceeds the whole?" Shabistari explains that Being is the part that resides and flows through all things. The appearance of the universe seems to be the 'whole' but is actually insubstantial and passing. He explains that what appears to be real "does not last two moments." Shabistari here introduces another of Ibn al-'Arabi's doctrines, that of the New Creation [*khalq jadīd*], the dissolution and recreation of the universe in each instant, unperceived by most people.

Shabistari now explores Sufi eschatology by explaining that there are three types of death. The first involves the New Creation and is happening in each moment. The second is the death at which a person can arrive through the annihilation of 'self.' This is a death of choice leading to liberation from the bondage of this world, and to the subsistence of God. The third is the death of the body which all creatures experience. The afterlife is thought to have two stages: the grave, and the Last Day. The 'grave' represents an intermediate existence in the Imaginal Realm, where souls continue to experience a psychic life not unlike dreaming. The Last Day represents the Resurrection, the final destination of souls. Our terrestrial actions will there be the making of our own heaven and hell. In the Resurrection, our earthly forms will re-emerge, but will conform completely to divine influence. As such, the existence of the Resurrection must be one of great bliss for those whose natures were selfless, and of great hardship and pain for those whose natures stabilized on selfishness, covetousness, and cruelty.

*What is the part that exceeds the whole?*
*What is the Way to discovering that part?*

☙ REPLY ❧

*Know that Being is the part that exceeds the whole.*
*Parts usually make the whole, but here it's cockeyed.*

*All that exists is overt multiplicity*
*which has no unity except internally.*

*The Being of the whole appeared through multiplicity.*
*Being flows through the inner unity of the part.*

635 *But in reality the whole has no existence*
*since it is ephemeral and derived from Reality.*

Since the whole's multiplicity is an appearance,
it is actually the lesser in relation to its part.

Existence has not become part of Necessary Being
since existence remains forever in its service.

Existence of the whole is the Single become multiple.
Through multiplicity It becomes ever more numerous.

The existent is named 'accident' because it's compounded.
The accident by its essential nature passes into nonbeing.

As each part of the whole returns to nonbeing,                    640
the whole in that moment becomes void of accidents.

Our universe is the whole and in every blink of the eye
it passes into nonbeing: "It doesn't last two moments."

Yet another universe is immediately created,
in every moment another earth and another sky.

In every moment a youth becomes an old man.
With every breath is an assembling and dissolution.

Worldly things do not abide more than two instants.
In the moment they die they are again born.

But this is not "the great calamity," the end of the world      645
which is the Last Day while this is the day of His works.

Take heed, there is a great difference between them,
so do not fall into misunderstanding this.

Look carefully at particularity and totality.
Examine the hour and day, the month and year.

◈ ILLUSTRATION ◈

If you want to understand the meaning of this,
see how you are subject to death and life.

Everything in this world from below to above
has a likeness in your body and spirit.

650   The world is an individual person like you.
You became its spirit and it is your body.

Human beings have three kinds of death.
The first occurs in every moment of one's essence.

Second is the death one can choose to die.
Third is the compulsory death affecting all.

Since death and life are related to each other,
there are also three human lives at three levels.

The chosen death is not known to worldly creation.
Out of all of creation only you can know it.

But the world changes in each moment,           655
and each moment's end is like its genesis.

All signs that are to appear at the Resurrection
can be seen at the time of your death agony.

Your body is like earth with your head as the sky.
Your senses are stars and the sun is your spirit.

Your bones are like mountains, rough and hard.
Vegetation is your hair and trees are your limbs.

Your dying body, full of regret
will tremble like the earth of the Apocalypse.

Your brain will reel and your spirit grow dark       660
as your senses flicker like shimmering stars.

From your pores will flow rivers of sweat
in which you'll drown and your body be lost.

As life slips away from you, my poor fellow,
your bones will go limp as wool fibers.

Twisted together your legs will be wound.
All pairs will be pried apart and left alone.

When the spirit has separated from its body
your earth will be featureless as "a leveled plain."

665   The world will go through the same changes
      that you will experience at the moment of dying.

      The subsistence of God is real, all else passes away.
      The whole matter is explained in Koranic verses.

      They inform that "All of this world is perishing"
      and reveal that "He is bringing a new creation."

      The creation and annihilation of the two worlds
      are like the creation and resurrection of human souls.

      Creation is constantly renewed in fresh creation,
      even through the seeming continuity of a long life.

670   God's effusions of bounty and grace expand
      from His intention to His Self-manifestation.

      On one side is His creating and completing.
      On the other is each moment's change in renewal.

      Yet when this sensible world passes away,
      all will remain in the next world,

      since everything you see is necessarily
      of two worlds: one, spirit and the other, form.

      Joining to the latter world is really a separation
      but with the spiritual world, "what is with God endures."

When manifestations conform with the Manifesting,     675
in the First will be shown the essence of the Last.

The Enduring is a name of absolute Being,
yet it resides wherein the Real flows and manifests.

All of the potentials from the house of this world
will suddenly manifest in the Next World.


∾ FORMULATION ∾

Any action that you originate and carry out
will be easier when repeated several times.

Each time whether for gain or loss
will leave a small trace in your soul.

Through habit, passing states become one's disposition,     680
just as over time fruit ripens to sweetness.

That's how people learn their varied trades.
That's how they create their thoughts and worries.

The actions and states that have left their traces
will be clearly apparent on the Last Day.

When you're stripped naked of body's garment,
your faults and talents will suddenly appear.

You'll have a body free of impurity
that reflects images like limpid water.

685   What's in your conscience will be apparent there.
Consider the verse, "All secrets will be unveiled."

Then, conforming to the plan of that special world,
qualities will be embodied as particular entities.

Just as the potentials of the elements here
gave rise to the three earthly natures,

all of your qualities will in the world of Spirit
become either beautiful lights or raging fires.

Individual nature will vanish from existence.
There won't remain any sense of above and below.

690   You will have no death in the House of Eternal Life.
Your original form and your soul will rise there as one.

Your limbs and eyes will become [perceptive] as your heart.
They'll be purified of the darkness of earthly form.

The Light of the Real will manifest in you.
Your unlimited sight will behold the Real.

You will have shattered the two worlds to oblivion.
I don't know how great will be your ecstasy.

Consider the verse, "Their Lord gives them to drink."
Of what [wine of] purity? One washing away the self.

O what a wine! What pleasure and deep savor!                    695
O what wealth! What rapture and passion!

How very sweet the moment we're less the self,
become fabulously rich though mere dervishes.

No religion, no mind, no piety, no understanding,
fallen drunk and completely senseless in the dust!

How measure paradise, heavenly maidens, or eternity?
There's no room for strangers in Unity's sanctuary.

Though I've seen this vision and drunk of this wine,
I don't yet know what will come afterwards.

After every drunken bout is a hangover.                         700
At this thought my heart fills with regret.

Shabistari here revisits a perplexing problem that is resolved through mystical unveiling: the seeming separation of God and the world, or as he puts it here, the Eternal and the temporal. The Eternal and the temporal are not actually separate but are really one event. The temporal is nonbeing whose only reality is in the form of the 'immutable essences' of all things [al-aʿyān al-thābita], existing beyond time and space in the knowledge of the Real. The Eternal on the other hand is God, the Real, who acts on His knowledge through the Divine Names and Acts to create the world around us. It is our own misperception that gives rise to the illusion of our separate existence.

Each immutable essence becomes a locus of manifestation [maẓhar] for a Name because it happens to have the latent predisposition for that Name. The Names should be conceived as relationships. We can understand the matter by analogy if we consider a man. When he marries, we say that he is a husband and when he has a child, we call him a father. The man's names are potential relationships rather than absolute characteristics. Similarly, God's Names appear within corresponding loci. Beyond the Names is the pure Essence of the Real. Yet within each of the Names, as its root, is the Essence. So all Names actually refer to their Essential Origin. The temporal's existence can only be called 'contingent' since it has no true existence of its own, being fully dependent on the Real for its appearance within existence.

✿ ✿ ✿

How did the Eternal and temporal become separate,
with the latter called the world and the former, God?


∾ REPLY ∾


The Eternal and temporal are not separate things
since it's through Being that nonbeing is sustained.

Eternal is the All while this other is like a phoenix.
But for the Real, all names would be fictitious.

It's impossible for nonbeing itself to become existent.
With regard to existence, Being is immutable.

The one does not become the other nor vice versa.                    705
Let all of this difficulty now be easy for you!

All of this world is an imagined existence
like the spinning point that appears to be a circle.

Go and spin the flame of a torch round and round
to see that the circle comes from spinning.

Though the number one must be used for counting,
its unity doesn't alter with the numbers mounting.

Cease talking of things "other than God."
Use a clear mind to distinguish unity from multiplicity.

710  How can you doubt that multiplicity is pure illusion?
That with Unity, duality is sheer impossibility?

Nonbeing like Being is exclusively unique.
All multiplicity has manifested through relativity.

Appearances of diversity and types of divine Self-expression
have arisen through the chameleon of contingent being.

Since the Being of every individual is One,
all bear witness to the oneness of the Real.

TRANSLATOR'S INTRODUCTION
TO THE THIRTEENTH INQUIRY

In this section, Shabistari explains some of the erotic imagery used by Sufis in their poetry and other writings. A reader may take this imagery to be mere romantic symbolism, but our poet explains that these words, such as 'eyes,' 'lips,' 'curl-tips,' and 'beauty-mark,' are actually representations and reflections from the World of Meanings ['ālam-i ma'ānī]. The World of Meanings can be thought of as a vast world of unlimited spiritual meanings, which are the inner reality of our world of forms.

Just as the human spiritual form is a comprehensive locus of manifestation for all of the Divine Names, the perfect human physical form is the visible showplace of celestial beauty and power. The Real, through the Names and Actions, manifests in spiritual meanings which Sufis apprehend in a state of ecstatic consciousness and 'spiritual tasting.' Sufi poets then write of their experiences using related earthly symbols. A problem arises when most people read or listen to such poetry, since few have had these experiences. Most people, hearing the words through the gross filters of the senses and the limited intellect, are unable to understand them rightly. Shabistari encourages the seeker to penetrate to the inner meaning as deeply as possible, to use the words to leap toward their inner meaning. He also advises that only those who have experienced self-annihilation, spiritual drunkenness and the overwhelming love of God can truly understand those words.

The first step is to comprehend the Sufis' hermeneutics [*ta'wīl*], of these symbols. The face or cheek represents the unmanifested Essence. The down covering the face signifies the immaterial individualized spirits in the World of Spirits, which is the first emanation from the Essence. The lips represent the Merciful Breath which breathes the 'Beautiful Qualities' onto creation and offers the possibility of intimacy with God. The eyes represent Divine self-sufficiency and independence from creation, and their glance expresses the Divine Wrath, annihilating all that is other than the unique Essence. The curls and tresses symbolize the actions and effects of the Names as they manifest in our world, veiling the Divine from creation. For this reason I have preferred the English 'locks' in translation, conveying the idea of tresses, and that of attachment as well.

The beauty mark on the Beloved's cheek represents the Unity of the Divine. All of the manifested worlds originate from that Unity which encompasses everything. The mystic's Heart is the only place in all of creation that is a reflection of that beauty mark. This is emphasized in the *ḥadīth qudsī*, "My heaven and earth contain Me not, but the Heart of My faithful servant contains Me."

Yet the Heart is in constant flux, its state changing from moment to moment. This is because it is also the locus for the relationships emanating from Unity, namely, the Divine Names. Hence, the mystic's experience fluctuates between spiritual expansion and contraction, ecstasy and grief, transcendent consciousness, then attachment.

It is this spiritual Heart which informs the mystic and acts as the interface [*barzakh*] between the world of meanings and the world of forms. This heart alone can appreciate the spiritual symbolism of Sufi poetry.

ᑐ THE THIRTEENTH INQUIRY ᑐ

*What does the gnostic intend to convey*
*by symbolic reference to the eyes and the lips?*

*To what does he aspire with tresses, down, and mole,*      715
*this man of mystical stations and states?*

ᑐ REPLY ᑐ

*All things that are visible in this world*
*are like reflections of the sun of That world.*

*The world is like the down, beauty-mark, curl, and brow.*
*Everything in its right place is beautiful.*

*Theophany is of Beauty and sometimes of Majesty.*
*The Face and tresses are symbols of those meanings.*

The attributes of High Truth include kindness and wrath.
Heart-idols' faces and curls reflect these two properties.

720   As the words come to our hearing through the senses,
      they are initially given sensual assignations.

      Yet the World of Meanings is not limited in this way.
      How can such limited words hope to reach it?

      An inner meaning revealed in 'spiritual tasting'
      is surely beyond the reach of words of approximation.

      When a man of the heart explains spiritual realities,
      he makes use of metaphors to convey their meaning.

      Things of the senses are shadows of the Other World.
      They are like an infant and That world suckles them.

725   In my view these metaphorical words
      should first apply to their spiritual meanings.

      Words took given meanings through vulgar usage
      but what do common folk know about inner meanings?

      Once they observed meanings in the world of intellect,
      from there they transferred the intent of the words.

      The thinker observed the intellectual relationships
      when seeing the words, thus the meanings descended.

But no totally suitable comparison is possible,
so rest from the struggle of trying to find one.

In this spiritual expression, no one can be your judge          730
as there is no spiritual authority here except the Real.

Yet while still ensnared by 'self,' beware, beware!
Hold to the code of the Law, take care!

People of the heart have license in three states:
Self-annihilation, spiritual drunkenness, and love's fervor.

The one who is familiar with these three states
knows the real meaning of words and their intention.

If you have not attained to these special states,
don't blaspheme in ignorance by your imitation.

The states known through the Real are not illusory          735
and not everyone will find the secrets of the Way.

Foolish talk, O friend, is not spoken by real mystics
who unveil the truth or confirm it inwardly.

I've spoken of the application of words and meanings.
May you come to understand this bewildering subject!

Look towards inner meanings in their ultimate sense.
Observe each of their properties, one by one.

Find similitude in the special aspect of each meaning;
Find transcendence in other aspects of its meaning.

740    As this principle has now been prescribed for you,
I will disclose more about these metaphors.

## THE SYMBOLISM
## OF THE EYES AND LIPS

Look at who appears in the eyes of the Witness.
Observe her characteristics in the Beyond.

From those eyes come lovesickness and ecstasy.
The essence of Being is revealed in those lips.

Her eyes leave hearts rapturous, in a stupor.
Those lips completely veil souls from themselves.

All hearts agitate and burn because of those eyes.
Those ruby lips restore health to lovesick souls.

745    Although this world seems unworthy of her gaze,
her lips breathe mercies on us in every moment.

One moment She turns to humanity and caresses hearts.
The next She brings relief to the hopeless.

Smiling, She brings to life this water and clay.
In that moment the skies burn with grief.

With every wink She sets a baited trap.
Her hinting glance becomes a wine tavern.

With a wink She gives existence over to plunder,
then with a kiss, She restores everything to order.

Her distant eyes keep our blood boiling.                    750
Her lips hold the soul in a drunken ecstasy.

She ravishes our hearts with flirtatious winks.
Her alluring lips expand our spirits.

Should you desire an embrace from her eyes and lips,
her eyes say "no" while her lips whisper "yes."

With a fierce glance She does away with the world.
Her kiss strokes the soul in every breath.

Just one wink and we give up the soul
and we're revived by one caress of those lips.

In a wink of the eye comes the end of the world.           755
Through a breathing of Spirit, the creation of Adam.

Once fretting over her eyes and ruby lips,
all the world made wine-worship their calling.

Yet the world cannot claim Existence in her eyes
since She sees it as a dream and a drunken vision.

All of our existence is either dream or rapture.
What link can this dust claim to the Lord of Lords?

Reason is stranded with a hundred confusions.
For whom is the verse, "Created under My loving eyes"?

〜 THE SYMBOLISM OF THE TRESSES 〜

760    Long and twisted are the tales of the Beloved's tresses!
       But what is right to say about this mysterious matter?

       Don't ask me to speak of those wavy curls.
       Don't shake the painful chains that bind the insane!

       Last night I was speaking plainly of her perfect stature
       when a curl-tip warned me, "Hide away this matter!"

       The wavy curls have overwhelmed straight truth,
       thus the way of the seeker has become confused.

       These locks have chained every heart [to multiplicity].
       All souls are in confused agitation because of them.

765    One hundred thousand hearts hang all around,
       and not one of them has been freed from its ringlet.

Were She to shake those fragrant tresses from her face,
not one impious soul would be left in the world.

Were She to hold them still so as to hide her face,
not one true believer would be left to existence.

Since her ringlets were intended as a snare
she parts them flirtingly to show a hint of her face.

If She were to snip her tresses, what harm of it,
since the shorter night would increase the day?

When She ambushed reason's caravan along the road, 770
her own hands secured the prisoner with ringlets.

Her locks are never for a moment at rest,
here showing the dawn and there bringing on the night.

In her curls and face are a hundred nights and days,
and countless wondrous games are found therein.

Adam's clay was kneaded and formed in that span,
and carries the musky fragrance of her tresses.

Our hearts retain the trace of her scented hair
so they cannot be at rest for even a moment.

I've renewed my struggle [with multiplicity] in each moment. 775
I have wrenched my heart out from myself.

The reason those locks have so troubled my heart
is that they hide the Face that set fire to my soul.

## THE SYMBOLISM
## OF THE FACE AND DOWN

Here the Face is a showplace of divine beauty.
Grandeur's threshold is intended by the down.

Her Cheek penned a hairlet's script within beauty:
"Except for Mine, there is no beautiful face."

The down is the green meadow of the world of the soul.
Some for that reason call it the Abode of Eternal Life.

780   Starting from her dark locks, make day into night.
From her down make your way to the Spring of Life.

Be like Khidr in his traceless station.
Absorb of the Water of Life like down's meadow.

If with certainty you gaze on her Face and down,
you will know Unity from multiplicity in each.

From her Face you will understand the world's workings.
Her down opens the book of inner mystery to your eyes.

Though another sees the down on her Face,
my heart gazes at her Face in that lovely down.

Yet her Face holds the mighty Seven Verses,                785
wherein each letter is a vast ocean of meaning.

Concealed under each hairlet of that lovely cheek,
are thousands of oceans of knowledge from the Unseen.

See the heart's mirror and the Throne of the Merciful
in the beauty of the down and Face of the Beloved.

꙰ THE SYMBOLISM ꙰
꙰ OF THE CHEEK'S BEAUTY-MARK ꙰

On that Face is a beauty-mark so simple and vast,
the original center of creation's circumference.

Its line completely circles the two worlds,
the life and pleasure of Adam's soul and heart.

For that dark mole the heart suffers and pains                790
by being the reflected image of that beauty-mark.

That mole holds the heart in its agitated state;
There's no escaping the suffering of this state.

Multiplicity can never enter within Unity.
Two points can't exist within essential Unity.

I'm not sure if her beauty mark is my heart's reflection
or if my heart mirrors the mark on that lovely Face,

if my heart came from the reflection of her mole,
or if the reflection of the heart is manifesting There.

795    Whether heart is on her Face or She within the heart
is a secret that is utterly concealed from me.

Yet if this heart of mine is the mirror of her mole,
why should I have so many varied states?

My heart can be rapturous from her intoxicating glance,
sometimes moved to agitation like her shaking locks.

At times it's as luminous as her moonlike Face.
Sometimes it darkens to the blackness of her tresses.

My heart is a holy mosque then a synagogue.
Sometimes it's a hell and then paradise.

800    At times my heart soars above the seven heavens
then it falls to beneath this heap of dirt.

After a time of renunciation and humble devotion
it is time for wine, the lamp, and the Witness.

[ 144 ]

❖ ❖ ❖

In Shabistari's reply to the thirteenth inquiry, he explains how
certain symbols used by Sufis pertain to mystical experience
in the 'World of Meanings' ['ālam-i ma'ānī]. The fourteenth
inquiry introduces terminology describing the mystical
experiences leading to *fanā'*, the self-annihilation in the
vastness of God. First, he explains that 'wine,' 'candle-flame,'
and 'Witness' are all Self-disclosures of the Real. As such,
they have the same inner meaning. He then illustrates how
mystical experiences differ from each other. His simile, based
on the Koran's famous *Verse of Light* [24:35], is that of a
traditional lamp, a taper burning within a glass-sheltered
niche.

When human consciousness turns its attention inward,
toward the Real and away from the world, the first thing
to be experienced is rapture and the vision of photisms and
luminous forms. These luminous theophanic forms are
represented by the light coming through the colored and
patterned glass protecting the lamp. These initial visions
and experiences bring about desire in the seeker for intimacy
with the Real. Deepening mystical experience reveals a
purer light, the spiritual taste [*dhawq*] that heralds gnosis
and true spirituality. Finally there is the pure beauty of the
'Witness' which is a theophany of the Essence of the Real.

This is represented by the 'bright rays of spirits,' which are the first manifestation from the Essence.

'Wine' is often used as a symbol of annihilation of the self, an emptiness and loss of the normal self-identified consciousness, which occurs initially for short intervals during the mystical practice of *dhikr,* the sincere invocation of God's name. This leads, as revealed in the Koran, to a turning of the Divine Attention towards the inner self of the mystic, and hence to the experience of God within the consciousness. The Real 'drowns' the self-identity of the mystic in progressively finer theophanies, which are called 'annihilation of the actions,' 'annihilation of the attributes,' and finally, 'annihilation of the essence.' A central feature of self-annihilation is the experiential realization of the Oneness of God.

The 'wine-tavern' symbolizes Unity. 'Tavern drunkard' is a consciousness that operates beyond all relations and dualities within the vast ocean of Unity. As Shabistari points out, the tavern drunkard is beyond judgments of good and evil, and disgrace and good name. He is beyond qualities and characteristics, and beyond the initial relationship to a teacher, which had existed for the purpose of cleansing the disciple of egotism and error.

Mention is made of the *samā',* the audition of music and participation in dance, a part of the Sufi tradition involving the inducement of ecstatic consciousness. Shabistari endorses these practices, but indicates that *samā'* finds its reality in the spirit. As such it is intended for practicing mystics, not those who merely dance with the hope of some attainment.

Rumi and other Sufis likewise warn that only those purified of their selfishness may benefit from the *samāʿ*.

*What are the meanings of wine, candle-flame, and Witness?*
*What is intended by the words, "being a tavern drunk?"*

❦ REPLY ❦

*Wine, candle, and Witness are of one meaning*
*since every form is a Self-disclosure of God.*

*Wine means ecstasy, and candle mystical 'tasting.'*          805
*Gaze on the Witness who is hidden from no one.*

*Wine means the glass case, candle the lamp inside,*
*witness the bright rays emanating from spirit.*

*Sparks of the Witness burned in the heart of Moses.*
*His wine was the fire and his candle that glowing bush.*

*Wine and candle are the spirit and light of the ascension,*
*but the beautiful Witness is His greatest sign.*

Wine, candle and Witness are all present,
so don't be absent from delighting in beauty!

Come drink the wine of selflessness for a time
to find safety from the tight grip of self.

810    Drink the wine that will release you from self
so the drop's existence may be joined to the sea.

Drink this wine whose goblet is the Beloved's Face.
The cup is the pure eye of that Drunkard.

Search for a wine poured in neither cup nor bowl,
a wine-drinking wine, a drinker of cupbearers!

Drink wine from the cup of his Everlasting Face.
"Their Lord gave them to drink" is a true cupbearer.

Pure is the wine that from the stain of existence
washes you clean with a time of pure drunkenness.

815    Drink wine! Free yourself from cold-heartedness.
This drunkenness is better than being a 'good man.'

For one fallen so far from God's Court,
veils of darkness are better than veils of light.

See how Adam was blessed a hundredfold by darkness
while Satan was damned forever despite knowing light.

If the heart's mirror is thoroughly polished,
of what benefit if it only reflects your 'self'?

When a ray from his Face shines into the wineglass,
countless effervescent bubbles form in its draught!

The World of Spirit bubbles up in this wine                    820
making bubbles like domes over the Friends of God.

The Universal Intellect is ecstatic from this wine
while the Universal Soul wears the earring of a slave.

All of this world is just his tavern.
The heart of each atom is another of his cups.

Reason is drunk, angels are drunk, and spirit is drunk.
Even the atmosphere is drunk, as are earth and sky!

Heaven spins bewildered and searching in ecstasy,
its heart's desire is for one whiff of God's scent.

The angels have drunk a pure wine from a clean cup        825
and poured the dregs down onto this earth.

This one drink has left the elements gay and tipsy,
sometimes falling in water and sometimes in fire.

From a whiff of this wine which was spilled to earth,
man extracts himself and makes for the heavens.

The wineglass reflection stirs spirit in his withered body.
From its shining rays, frozen spirit is enlivened.

All the Earth's creatures are forever tipsy from it,
traveling far from their homes in their searching.

830   One, from a whiff of the dregs, becomes a great thinker.
Another, from its pure color, a transmitter of lore.

One from half a draught becomes a sincere seeker.
Another who drinks the whole flask is a burning lover.

Yet another guzzles in one amazing gulp, swallowing
wine and tavern along with drinker and Cupbearer!

He's drunk down all and his mouth remains open!
What an oceanic heart has this great libertine!

He has absorbed all of existence in this one gulp.
He's found freedom from both affirming and denying.

835   He is free of the need for dry austerities and idle talk
but holds to the garment of the tavern sage.

To be a tavern drunkard means to be freed of 'self.'
Self is blasphemous even if thinking itself pious.

From the wine tavern comes a guiding sign:
"Unity means dropping all relativities."

The wine tavern is of the world beyond analogy.
It is the station of carefree, brazen lovers.

The wine tavern is the nest of Spirit's bird.
It is a threshold opening onto the Placeless.

The drunkard is effaced within effacement.                    840
In his vast desert, the world is a mirage.

This tavern condition is without limits or extremes
where neither beginnings nor ends can be seen.

If your search there lasts one hundred years,
you'll neither yet find yourself nor another.

This tavern crowd is without feet, without heads.
None of them are believers or heretics.

The wine of selflessness has gone to their heads.
They've abandoned all sense of good and evil.

845    *All drank this wine with neither mouth nor lips,*
        *finding freedom there from disgrace and good name,*

        *free from ecstatic utterances, visions and states,*
        *and imaginings from retreats, austerities and miracles.*

        *A whiff of the dregs of that wine and all is given up.*
        *From the taste of annihilation all are in rapture.*

        *Dervish staff, bowl, prayer beads, and toothbrush*
        *have all been gambled away for those dregs.*

        *Falling into water, then rising through mud,*
        *in place of tears they weep their own blood.*

850    *They are sometimes enraptured in Love's world,*
        *holding their necks out like swift racers.*

        *They sometimes gaze at the wall with dark faces,*
        *then are blissfully rosy-cheeked awaiting the hangman.*

        *Finding Love's passion in the dervish dance,*
        *they spin headless and limbless like the turning heavens.*

        *With every tune played by the samāʿ musicians,*
        *a deep rapture reaches them from the Other World.*

        *Samāʿ is spirit, not just melody and words.*
        *In each musical scale is a unique, subtle secret.*

In ecstasy they pull off the ten-layered garment,                    855
freeing themselves of all qualities of color and scent.

They wash away in a draught of that purest wine
all remaining color of black, green and blue.

Having drunk one cup of that pure, special wine
makes one a Sufi purified of all qualities.

They've swept from their souls the filth of a dung-heap,
and don't tell a hundredth of what they've seen.

They hold to the garments of drunken libertines,
weary now of talk of the Shaikh and discipleship.

What is the meaning of the Shaikh and disciple's bond?          860
What are austerities and piety but pure deception?

If your vision is still fixed on differences of quality,
better for you are the idol, belt, and Christianity.

In Islam idolatry is forbidden. As a result, Islamic art usually finds its expression in geometric and calligraphic forms. There are exceptions, (e.g. miniature painting and the use of animal motifs in decoration), but these are usually kept far from mosques and other places of worship. In the fifteenth inquiry, Shabistari broaches the subject of idolatry. First, the Sufis hold the view that most religious people are actually idolaters. Theirs is an idolatry of institutions and religious ideas leading to unconscious self-love and self-deception. Second, mystical experience reveals that the Real is the cause of all things, including idols. Moreover, It permeates them and is their essential nature on the side of Being. Apart from this, idols and all other things are sheer nonbeing and could not manifest even as visible entities. So all things are actually 'faces of God' as revealed in the Koranic verse "Wherever you turn, there is the face of Allah"(2:115).

The ultimate iconoclasts of Islamic society, the Sufis have sometimes so infuriated the conventionally religious that they become the target for verbal and physical abuse, and even for officially sanctioned murder. Shabistari carries on the tradition of iconoclasm in his reply and quotes several passages from the Koran that are conveniently ignored by his rigid religious brethren.

He proceeds with a poetic investigation of sincerity and hypocrisy and spiritual teachership. Shabistari asks us to turn towards our conscience, our usual relationships and our expectations and desires. He evaluates the behavior of false teachers. He uses terms such as *idol, belt* (the belt Christians wore to distinguish themselves from Muslims) – normally pejorative in his society – as symbols of praiseworthy spiritual qualities. He does so to turn the status quo of hypocrisy on its head so that the seeker can approach the spiritual path with greater sincerity.

He ends the *Garden of Mystery* with a section on the 'Christian Youth,' a symbol for the 'Teacher of the Age,' whose perfection is such as to make him a comprehensive mirror of God. It is because of the influence of such a perfect guide (or the guidance of the Real Itself) that our poet finds deliverance from his lower nature. His inner self awakened, Shabistari finds a garden of spirituality communicated from the heart of his spiritual guide. It is from that world that he brings to us the *Garden of Mystery*.

He asks the reader to study the poem carefully, claiming that it is a unique expression of spirituality, not previously articulated by anyone. In the *Garden of Mystery* he has combined the religious, the philosophical, and the gnostic into what he regards as a "precise science." He ends the work by asking the reader to seek God's blessing on him.

*In this alley-way the idol, Christian belt and Christianity*
*are infidelity – or if not, say then what are they?*

*The idol here means the theophany of Love and Unity;*
*Tying the belt represents the pledge to service.*

*Since infidelity and faith are both sustained in Being,*
*unity's work is the same as idol worship.*

865 *Since all things are manifestations of Being,*
*surely at least one of them must be an idol?*

*Consider this well, O thoughtful man:*
*The idol as an aspect of Being cannot be invalid.*

*Know that God Most High is this idol's creator.*
*Whatever has issued from Goodness is itself good.*

*Being, wherever it is, is entirely good.*
*If there be any evil, that is otherness, it's nonbeing.*

*If a Muslim knew what an idol really was,*
*he would know there is faith in idol worship.*

If the polytheist were aware of the truth of his idol,       870
how could he have gone astray in his worship?

He has seen nothing in his idol but its created form,
and for that reason is a heretic in the Faith.

You also, if you don't see within its hidden Truth,
cannot be counted as a Muslim in the Faith.

Weary of the superficial and outward form of Islam
are those for whom "real infidelity" has become apparent.

Within every idol is hidden Spirit.
Hidden within infidelity is True Faith.

Infidelity is ever reciting the worship of God.       875
"All things praise Him" is proof of this.

What should I say if some think I've lost my way?
"Say Allah, and leave them to vain sport and play."

Who adorned the idol's face with such beauty?
If the Real had not willed it, who could be an idolater?

He acts, and He speaks, and He is!
He does good, He speaks the good, He is good.

See One, say One, and know One.
This summarizes the root and branch of true Faith.

880    *I don't say this, go and hear it from the Koran's*
        *"No distinction among the creatures of the Merciful."*

### ∾ SYMBOLISM OF THE BELT ∾

*I've looked carefully, observing the origin of things.*
*The tying of the belt signifies service and obedience.*

*The people of Knowledge are not trusting of a word*
*unless they have known its original sense.*

*Tie the hero's belt of obedience like a real man.*
*Come be among those who "Keep your pledge to Me."*

*On the steed of knowledge with the mallet of worship*
*carry off the ball of felicity from the polo field.*

885    *This is the reason for which you were created*
        *out of all the many other creatures He created.*

*Knowledge is like a father and good works a mother*
*of countless states that are a "coolness for the eyes."*

*There is no person without a father in this world*
*save Jesus like whom there's never been another.*

*Abandon idle talk of visions, ecstatic exclamations,*
*the fantasy of inner lights, and doing miracles.*

Your miracles are found in the worship of God.
Except for that it's pride, hypocrisy, and vanity.

Except for the path of inner poverty                                890
all else is the cause of vanity and deceit.

From contemptible Satan, denier of the Real,
come thousands of wonders defying nature.

He manifests through the walls, sometimes the roof,
sometimes he's in the heart, sometimes the body.

He is ever manifesting hidden states within you.
He brings about heresy, transgression, and rebellion there.

Iblis is a [false] prayer-leader bowing in front of you
but when will your wonders ever be on a par with his?

If your wonders are done for personal show,                        895
you're then like Pharaoh boasting claims of divinity.

The person who is truly acquainted with the Real
never does a thing for the sake of personal show.

Beware if your face is turned to people.
Don't let yourself be captured in this way.

Sitting with the vulgar, you undergo metamorphosis,
but one leading from a higher to a lower state.

[ 159 ]

Do not interact nor keep company with the vulgar
lest you suddenly find your inner nature overwhelmed.

900    You've wasted your lovely life in futility.
Don't you ask what this kind of life will amount to?

Fretting in the assembly of those of high-sounding titles,
they've chosen an ass for a leader, but look at his beard!

Leadership has now fallen to the completely ignorant.
That is how people have reached such a sad state.

Examine the one-eyed Dajjal that you may understand
how examples [of ignorance] have arrived in the world.

See another example, O man of inner feeling,
in his donkey whose name is Jassas.

905    See all of these donkeys in the pack of Jassas.
He is their leader on the path of ignorance.

Our master Muhammad related stories of the end of time
and gave clear signs of the end in several anecdotes.

See how in these days the blind and deaf are shepherds.
All the sciences of true Faith have flown to the skies.

There no longer remains any courtesy or modesty.
See how no one is ashamed of his own ignorance.

[ 160 ]

All the conditions of the world have been inverted.
If you have a mind, take a look at what has happened.

One who would be cursed, rejected, and despised                    910
is now a shaikh because his father was a pure man.

Khidr, the hidden guide, killed that wicked son
whose fathers were saintly and unworthy of disgrace.

Now with this 'shaikh' of yours you've become a real ass.
In stupidity he is a bigger donkey than you are!

Since he cannot tell a foe from a friend,
how will he purify your inner consciousness?

And if the son were to have the signs of his father,
what can be said except that it's "light upon light."

That son who is of good counsel and good behavior             915
is like the choicest fruit and the purpose of a tree.

And yet how can a shaikh of the Faith come from one
who can't tell good from bad, or evil from good?

Being a seeker means to learn the knowledge of Faith.
The lamp of the heart will thereby be illuminated.

None has ever learned this from the dead.
A lamp cannot be lit from ashes.

[ 161 ]

I've realized in my heart that for this work,
I should bind around myself the Christian belt.

920    This is not so that I'll gain a wide reputation.
I have that already and it's cause for shame.

As some associates in this work have become vile,
my obscurity would be better than their renown.

Again an inspiration comes to me from the Real:
Don't fault wisdom for the existence of fools.

Why, if there were no scavengers in our lands,
there would be an awful mess for the rest of creation.

Differences in predisposition explain different associations.
That is the way of this world, and God knows best.

925    Yet keep yourself distant from the company of fools.
If you really want to worship, break with habit.

Habit and norm do not go with real worship;
Perform sincere worship and abandon custom.

I *have seen that Christianity's aim is real detachment.*
I've *seen it as the breaking of the bonds of imitation.*

*Sacred Unity's courtyard is the monastery of Spirit*
*where the Simurgh of the Everlasting makes Its nest.*

*From God's Spirit, Jesus, there appeared detachment*
*since he was manifested from the sacred Spirit.*

*There is also a spirit from God within you*          930
*in which is found the Most Holy's trace.*

*If you seek the extinction of the earthly self,*
*come into the Presence of Divinity.*

*Whoever has, like an angel, left the earthly soul*
*will rise Jesus-like, to the fourth celestial realm.*

### ILLUSTRATION

*A nursing infant has a restricted existence,*
*remaining cradled and close to its mother.*

*When he comes of age and is ready for travel,*
*if he's really a man, he'll travel with his father.*

935    *Earthly elements are your mother of the lower realm.*
*You are a child whose father is the celestial Father.*

*That is why blessed Jesus said at his ascension,*
*"I am in harmony with my Father who is above."*

*You too, spirit of your Father, go to your Father.*
*Your spiritual companions have left, so go.*

*If you really want to become a bird in flight,*
*throw this world's carcass to the vultures.*

*Give up this treacherous world to the base.*
*Decaying flesh is only fit for dogs.*

940    *What value your parentage? Seek harmony and balance.*
*Turn your face to the Real and abandon ties of lineage.*

*The one who dives deep into the sea of nonbeing*
*has the verse, "no ties between them that day," today.*

*Any relationship that comes about through lust*
*only results in pride and selfishness.*

*If lust were not the acting force between people,*
*all of these 'relationships' would appear as fables.*

*Since desire was the force working between them,*
*one became a mother and the other a father.*

I *don't say what are your father and your mother,* 945
*as you should live with them in cordial respect.*

*The deficient in thought has been named your sister.*
*The envious has been given the title of brother.*

*One's very enemy is called a child.*
*A complete stranger is considered as family.*

*Tell me who are your maternal and paternal uncles?*
*What is gained from them except pain and sorrow?*

*As to your friends on the mystic path,*
*they may be friends but they also seek amusement.*

*If you pause for a moment to think about them,* 950
*you will see what I am trying to explain.*

*All are as a fable, a spell, and a burden for you.*
*By the soul of Master Muhammad, all are a mockery.*

*Abandon your self like the courageous ones,*
*yet do not transgress the rights of anyone.*

*If you neglect any detail of the Law,*
*you'll be detained from Faith in both worlds.*

*Don't violate the strictures of the Law,*
*yet take care of your own inner needs.*

955     Gold and women are the source of sorrow.
       Put them aside like Jesus, the son of Mary.

       Become a 'ḥanīf,' free from restrictions of sect.
       Come into the monastery of Faith like a monk.

       As long as your vision beholds traces of otherness,
       your being in a mosque is like being in a church.

       If your veil of 'otherness' is lifted away,
       the monastery's form will become a mosque.

       It doesn't matter what state you're in,
       oppose your inverted self and find deliverance.

960     Idol and belt, Christian and church bell
       are all symbols of rejecting fame and good name.

       If you want to become one of the Special Servants,
       become prepared for sincerity and ethical behavior.

       Go and pull yourself from the way of selfishness;
       at every moment renew your faith in selflessness.

       Since our hidden selves are the real infidels,
       don't be satisfied with an outer worship of Islam.

       With every new moment turn to refresh your faith.
       Be a Muslim, be a Muslim, yes, be a Muslim!

Plenty of real faith is born of infidelity.                    965
Don't call that which increases faith infidelity.

Abandon vain hypocrisy, renown and name!
Leave the dervish cloak and tie the Christian belt.

Like our Sage, through idolatry be a transcendent one;
if you're human, give your heart to a [perfect] human.

Disengage yourself from all acceptance and rejection.
Give your heart at once to that Christian Youth.


### SYMBOLISM OF THE IDOL
### AND THE CHRISTIAN YOUTH

This idol of a Christian Youth is a manifest light,
a light that shines in the faces of these idols.

He is in the service of all hearts he enthralls.            970
Sometimes he's a minstrel, sometimes a cupbearer.

What a minstrel, who with just one lovely tune
sets fire to the proud harvest of one hundred ascetics!

What a cupbearer, who with just one overflowing cup
renders senseless two hundred sages of seventy years!

Drunk, he enters the dervish hospice at night
revealing their outbursts and incantations as fables.

And if he slips into the mosque at dawn,
he leaves not a man there aware of himself.

975 When he sneaks veiled and drunken into the college,
the professor of religion falls into a helpless stupor.

For love of him ascetics have fallen into helplessness.
They have given up hearth and home to become vagrants.

He makes one a true believer and another a heretic
thereby filling the world with struggle and evil.

Ecstasy's wine taverns are built of his lips.
The mosques are lit by his brilliant face.

He has made possible all of my strivings.
Through him I've seen my heathen self die.

980 My heart had a hundred veils of learning and knowledge,
veils of selfishness, pride, hypocrisy, and imaginings.

That lovely dawn moon came in through my door,
waking me from heedlessness and making me aware.

His face illumined the spirit's sanctuary within me.
Through him I came to know who I really am.

When I looked for a time at that awesome face,
a sigh arose from the depths of my soul.

He said to me: "O impostor and hypocrite,
you have spent your life seeking renown!"

"Look at your learning, devotions, pride and imaginings.            985
O unaccomplished one, who detained you from me?"

"Gazing at my face for but one half an hour
is worth more than a thousand years of worship!"

In short, the face of that world embellisher
revealed me to myself fully in that moment.

My soul's face was blackened with shame
at the thought of my lost life and my idleness.

When that moon turned his sun-like face my way
and saw that I had been cut off from hope,

he filled a cup of pure drink and handed it over,            990
which from his pure water lit a flame in me.

Now he said: "Of this wine without color and scent,
wash away the designs on the tablet of existence."

Sated completely from that pure wine-cup,
I fell from ecstasy into the dust.

Neither nonexistent nor existent in 'self';
I'm neither sober, nor tipsy, nor fully drunk.

At times like the Beloved's eyes I'm rapturous.
Sometimes I'm disturbed as her agitating locks.

995  I'm sometimes in the furnace of my lower nature,
sometimes in the garden from seeing her Face.

I've brought back this small share of the garden
and named it the Garden of Mystery.

Its flowers are the heart's hidden secrets,
secrets no one else has shared 'til now.

Lilies' tongues there speak of True Reality,
and narcissus eyes all see the Truth.

Consider all of this with the heart's insight
until all doubt has lifted from you.

1000  Look at the religious, philosophical, and gnostic
together refined into a precise science.

Don't read this work with contentious eyes
lest these flowers become thorns in your view.

Ingratitude is the mark of real ignorance.
Knowledge of Truth comes about through gratitude.

It was my hope in presenting this that the dear reader
would remember me with "Mercy be upon him!"

I invoke my own name's meaning to end this work.
O God, make me at last 'worthy of praise.'

**2** For the sake of translation into English, the masculine pronoun has been used. There is no gender implied in the Persian, and in Islam it is understood that God is incorporeal and without characteristics such as gender.

**3** *Kaf* and *nun* are the Arabic letters used in the Persian text which spell *kun!*, the command to "Be!," God's command for the origin of our cosmos. There is a play on the sound and symbolism of Arabic letters throughout the *Gulshan-i rāz*.

**4** *Qaf* is the Arabic letter which begins the words *qodrat,* or power, and *qalam,* the pen. This line refers to concepts of power and receptivity found in Islam and Sufism that are similar to those of Neoplatonic mysticism.

**5** The two worlds are the material and the spiritual, or this world and the hereafter.

**8** Shabistari is summarizing a complex process whereby the goal of creation is realized with the 'Completed Human' who, having made his or her way to the Source of existence, returns to the world with a modified consciousness, aware of the unity of all of existence.

**10** This refers to the Sufi doctrine of 'renewed creation,' developed by Ibn al-'Arabi. It is held that there is, in all life and creation, an oscillation between existence and non-existence at each moment. Lahiji, author of the most authoritative commentary on the *Gulshan-i rāz,* writes that this oscillation exists as God destroys and renews creation in each moment.

**15** Shabistari makes frequent use of the circle for analogy. Emerging from Absolute Being, creation enters the time/space universe and makes a 'descent' further and further away from Unity until it reaches a possibility in humanity of completing the circle, closing it again at Godhead.

**18** The Prophet Muhammad is considered to be not only the last of those chosen for prophetic mission, but also the first, since it is held that God created the reality of the prophets in pre-eternity, and that Muhammad was pre-eminent among them. In one *ḥadīth,* the Prophet said, "I was a prophet while Adam was yet between water and clay."

**19** *Aḥad* means in Arabic the Absolute Unity. In the Arabic spelling of Ahmad, another name for Muhammad, there is the addition of one letter, M. Muhammad represents the Completed Human, wherein are manifested the Divine Names, or relative characteristics of God.

**20** Koran 12:108.

**21** *Jamʿ-i jamʿ* or 'union of union' (all-comprehensive gatheredness) is the stage of experientially knowing the union of all things on the plane of *baqāʾ,* subsistence in God. This means that the union of all things is seen not only internally within the consciousness of the mystic, but externally in the world as well. There is another union before this stage on the plane of *fanāʾ,* or self-annihilation, where all things become one internally.

**25** The reference here is to Mansur al-Hallaj, a famous Sufi put to death for allegedly uttering such a heresy.

**26** Lahiji says that this outer knowledge is the religious shariat, or Law, which is like a dry shore.

**29** A detailed explanation of the use of these symbols is to be found in the latter chapters of the *Gulshan-i rāz.*

**32** The Hejira refers to the flight of the Prophet Muhammad from Mecca to Medina because of persecution. The Muslim calendar starts from that time. Shawwal is the name of one of the lunar months in the Arabic year. 717 in that calendar corresponds to 1317 AD.

**33** An area that now corresponds to northeastern Iran and northern Afghanistan. The reference is, in this case, specifically to Herat, Afghanistan.

**34** This great Sufi, Rukn al-Din Amir Husseini Herawi, often referred to in literature as Mir Husseini, died in 1318 AD. Several biographical accounts of him exist, including one in the *Sharḥ Gulshan-i rāz* by Muhammad Lahiji, used throughout my translation as a primary reference.

A *mathnawi* is a collection of rhyming couplets.

**57** This refers to the *Diwan,* or collection of poems, of Farīd al-Dīn ʿAṭṭār, a famous Sufi poet who lived in Nishapur, Iran, a couple of generations before Shabistari.

**72** The Real, *al-Ḥaqq,* is God. This name refers to the Divine as absolutely unqualified.

**80** The word used, *ta'yīd,* means both assistance and confirmation. This means that the reflection requires mystical experience and divine assistance.

**82** Koran 28:30. This is the Valley of Ayman where Moses met with God.

**87** Necessary and contingent are words taken into Islamic philosophy from the Classical Greeks. They mean respectively real Being, or God, and phenomenal being.

**96** Lahiji writes that the kernel is the sun, and the skin the world. The Real is like the sun overhead for someone sitting under a roof. If that sun did not move, one would only know that there was light, but not the origin of the light, since no change in its source could be perceived. One might think that the world had luminosity as one of its own properties.

**106** The Rationalists are the Mu'tazilites, a splinter group in early Islam that denied the possibility of seeing God either in this world or the next. Shabistari says that they are inwardly like the blind-born, incapable of spiritual vision.

**108** The word for taste [*dhawq*] refers to inner experience of God, or experience of the spiritual meanings within creation.

**112** Lahiji has clarified Shabistari's answer to the question in the following way: "The answer starts by referring to a *ḥadīth* (saying) of the Prophet: Think on the blessings of God, not on his Essence. In other words, think of God's mercies and not of His Essence. This refers to manifestations of the Names, Attributes, and divine Acts, which are the source of such blessings, visible and invisible. The remembrance of His mercies can be considered as a condition for the seeker because they allow him or her to pass from complete forgetfulness to alertness or partial awakening. Gratitude is therefore incumbent on the seeker for these mercies and increases them, whereas thanklessness is a sign of unbelief. However, such inquiry into the Essence of God is a sin because the infinite and universal character of the divine Essence is such that except for God Himself, none may attain to true knowledge of it.

"Thinking about the Essence is therefore a source of separation from Him. The Divine Essence refers to Absolute Existence. To look for a proof within thought or in any exterior manner to know the Essence is vain because He is the first cause of all things. Moreover, the notion of God's existence is innate within the individual essences. This inherent perception is not compatible with reasoning, which can be considered as a veil hampering this intuitive knowledge. That is why it has been said: think not on the Essence. The place for thought is on the manifestations of His mercies."

**114** Lahiji writes: "The Knowers have said that he who wishes to understand the Essence by way of the Names, Attributes, and Acts is comparable to him who, in his sleep, sees images that do not conform to waking reality. Those who come to know the Names, Attributes, and Acts of God by way of the Essence are those who, firstly, on the path of mystical unveiling reach the plane of the Absolute and then descend again to the level of the Names and the Attributes. They have seen that it is the Absolute Essence in Its perfection, which manifests everywhere through Names and Attributes. These mystics may be compared to those who are wide-awake and who perceive the reality of things."

**118** Gabriel, *Jibrīl* in Arabic, is the angel who revealed the Koran to the Prophet Muhammad and taught him the Muslim prayer.

**119** Islam holds that humanity has a greater capacity to know God than angels do. The Sufi Ibn al-ʿArabi wrote that angels are each aware of their own state but are not aware of the states of the rest of creation. During the *miʿrāj*, Muhammad's famous visit into the heavens upon his winged steed Burak, the great prophet reached a station of such close communion with God that the angel Gabriel, who was accompanying him, had to stop and leave Muhammad to continue his ascent alone. Muhammad, representing all perfected humans, traveled mystically beyond what is possible for angels and it is held that the same holds true for the sincere mystic who is spiritually annihilated and absorbed in God.

**123** Lahiji writes: "Shabistari indicates here that when a visible object is very close, the physical eye cannot see it. It is the same with the interior, spiritual eye. When the seeker on the way to God, to arrive closer to Him, transcends the lights of the manifestations of the names and the Attributes and becomes capable of perceiving the theophany of the Divine Essence, the light of the latter theophany seems to the seeker to be a black light because of its proximity. The vision of the seeker blackens from this proximity."

**125** When the mystic approaches spiritual annihilation, he perceives the inability of his own understanding to make further progress. The only solution is to give way completely to the Real.

**126** The creature cannot be separated from his own contingency, which is his origin in nonbeing. For this reason, he is black-faced, without light of his own. "Allah is the best Knower" is quoted to describe the actual experience of mysticism: God alone knows God.

**127** Proximity to the Black Light of the Essence is the greatest communion of the mystic. Mystics of this grade sometimes wear black turbans and garments.

**129** Silence is better because words would not help one to understand experiences, which transcend language. These last few lines refer to theophanies of light within the consciousness of the mystic wayfarer, which expand the very limited understanding of God found in belief and imagination. These and other lines reveal Shabistari's affiliation with the Kubravi Sufis, who specialized in the cultivation and interpretation of such theophanies.

**133** Here Shabistari introduces one of the most profound and important doctrines of Sufism, the unreality of existence as explained through the simile of the mirror. As mentioned in the introduction, Shabistari had carefully studied the works of Ibn al-'Arabi, who uses the mirror analogy in several contexts. Lahiji comments that nonexistence is here used to mean the 'immutable essences' [*al-a'yān al-thābita*], contained within the Real's absolute knowledge. In that state, these immutable essences are non-existent originals of all things we think of as existent in this world. When these essences are in alignment with Absolute Existence, the resulting reflection is a relative existence, which is claimed to be the state of all things of this world. So it is the Real's brilliant reflection that is seen, not any true existence on the part of the immutable essences. This is the cosmological picture. The poetry is multidimensional and Shabistari is also referring to personal mystical experience here. Nonexistence in this interpretation is the experience of extinguishing thought and image and all other clutter of the mind focused in *dhikr*. When this nonexistence is achieved, the brilliant reflection of the Real is experienced in a number of theophanic forms, such as those mentioned in the earlier couplets of this chapter.

**137** As an immutable essence in God's knowledge, nonexistence is pure. When the Light of the Real shines on it, this produces a seemingly existent entity. The hidden treasure is Absolute Existence, which reveals a little bit of itself in this process, just as a portion of the sun's brilliance, though not the sun itself, is revealed in an intermediary reflecting object.

**138**  This refers to a very important *ḥadīth qudsī* (sacred tradition) wherein God says in reference to why he created humanity: "I was a hidden treasure and I longed to be known." One of the possibilities of the All Possible, is to be known to Himself through his creation. The great Sufi Ibn al-ʿArabi writes in this context that mankind is as a mirror to God and God a mirror to mankind.

**139**  Since the world, or universe as we would now think of it, is a reflected image, humanity must be thought of as the eye of that image. The eye can see all parts of the reflected image in the reflection just as a person's eye can see all of himself when looking into a mirror. All of these various parts are brought into relative existence thanks to the action of the Names of the Real, attributes such as Living, Seeing, Knowing, Powerful, and the like. All of these manifestations unite in the eye of the image, the Completed Human, who is to be seen as the summation of creation.

**141**  The human being brings all of the Names of God together in one entity, otherwise found scattered in the rest of the cosmos. This is the meaning of the idea of God creating Adam in his own form or likeness.

**143**  This refers to a *ḥadīth qudsī* in which Allah says, "My servant ceases not to draw closer to Me through his *nawāfil* (acts of worship beyond the Islamic requirements) until I love him; and when I love him I am his ears through which he hears by Me, and his eyes through which he sees by Me, and his tongue with which he speaks by Me, and his hand with which he takes by Me."

**144**  Everything in the universe has come about through the action of God's Names, which are qualities, and all of these qualities are linked to the Essence. Therefore the entire world mirrors itself, and each atom contains the brilliance of a hundred shining suns, that is, the potential of the Essence.

**150** There is a *ḥadīth qudsī* where God says "My earth and my heavens are not able to contain Me, yet the heart of My devout servant is able to contain Me."

**165** Lahiji writes that, because there are many worlds including worlds beyond the reach of the senses, Shabistari asks what you really know about the world. Most people know only what is obvious to them.

**167** The Simurgh is a mythical bird that represents the unitary Essence of the Real. It lives on Qaf mountain in a realm beyond our own.

**169** Koran 69:39.

**170** The towns of Jabulqa and Jabulsa are referred to in many stories and anecdotes from the Islamic world. Lahiji says that Jabulqa was a great city in the Orient that represents the world of the archetypes. Jabulsa faces Jabulqa in the Occident and is an intermediate realm where spirits go after the death of the body.

**172** This refers to the words of Ibn Abbas, a relative of the Prophet concerning his interpretation of the Koranic verse 65:12. Ibn Abbas said: "If I should explain this verse and the secrets which it contains, the people would stone me to death or at the very least say that I was a heretic." Most Sufis, including Shabistari, find inner meanings in the Koran through *kashf*, mystical unveiling. These meanings are sometimes at odds with the overt meanings, and may be concealed to avoid trouble with the religious authorities.

**177** Koran 101:5.

**190** Quoting Abraham who, in his search for the Absolute, rejected the gods of his forefathers and likened them to stars that set below the horizon. Koran 6:76.

**191** Shabistari quotes God's words to Moses from His manifestation as the burning bush.

**192** Koran 7:143.

**193** In Shabistari's time it was thought that amber acted as a magnet for straw, possibly because of static electricity.

**197** Umm Hani was the daughter of Abu Talib, the Prophet Muhammad's uncle. The Prophet's miraculous ascension into the heavenly realms (*mi'rāj*) started from the *sarai* (home) of Umm Hani, by some reports. This view has been debated since others believe it took place from the home of his wife, Aisha. Lahiji writes that this *sarai* is a symbol for the senses and the world. The second line of this couplet is an important statement attributed to the Prophet, describing his own purity and spirituality, allowing him to be so permeated by the Real that any who saw him also saw the Real.

ک
ق

**198** In the Persian, the letter *kaf* is used to indicate the "corner of the worlds" [*kunj-i kaunin*], meaning existence. In the second line the letter *qaf* indicates the "closeness of two bows' lengths" [*qurb-i qab-i qausin*]. This expression refers to the closeness of communion between the Prophet and God during the *mi'rāj*.

**199** Quoting the *ḥadīth*: "O God, show us things as they really are."

**200** Lahiji writes that the mystic who has witnessed God's Self-manifestation inwardly and outwardly then sees the world as a form of the Koran. In Arabic the word *āyah* means a verse and also a 'sign.' Many Sufis have made the connection between the Koran as a book of signs and the world as the Koran's outward expression.

**201** For Shabistari, 'accidents' and 'substance' represent the phenomenal building blocks of the universe which, are apparent but ultimately unreal. Accidents [*a'rāḍ*] are entirely dependent for their appearance on substance [*jowhar*] in most philosophical presentations, which are derived from Greek thought.

**202** These are two of the most important suras, or chapters, in the Koran. The *fātiḥa* means the opener, and is the opening chapter of the Koran. *Ikhlāṣ* means sincerity and purity; it refers to a very important chapter on the Unity of the Real, located almost at the end of the Koran. Lahiji writes of the various worlds held by mystics to be emanations of the unmanifested Essence. They relate to the Ptolemaic spheres of the cosmos preceded by the First Intellect and the First Soul.

**203** The Universal Intellect is the first emanation of Unity, a concept borrowed from Greek thought and supported in the Koran. *Bismillāh* is the first word of the Koran. It means, "In the name of Allah." The dot found under the B of the Arabic script stands for the original Unity of God.

**204** Koran 24:35. This is one of the most widely quoted verses in the Koran to support the mystical, illuminative perspective.

**205**(1) Koran 25:59. After the divine manifestations of non-corporeal emanations of the First Intellect and First Soul, comes the first of the corporeal manifestations as the 'great sphere' which is the Throne of the Merciful, the *'arsh,* which surrounds the Ptolemaic eight spheres.

**205**(2)  Koran 2:255. The *kursi,* or Footstool, is the eighth sphere, which surrounds all of known creation.

**206**  The sura of the seven verses is the *fātiḥa,* which is the opening of the Koran. In it God says "Praise be to Allah, the Lord of the worlds," here interpreted to mean the manifested worlds taking form as the seven heavens or spheres.

**208**  The elements in the previous couplet are earth, air, water, and fire. The three-born (born of the four elements) are mineral, vegetable and animal.

**209**  Man, the microcosm of the cosmos, containing all of its possibilities, is the last to appear. *Surat al-Nās,* "Mankind," is the last chapter of the Koran.

**210**  'Horizons' refers to a statement in the Koran (41:53) "We will show them Our signs on the horizons [outside of themselves] and within their souls, until it becomes clear that He is the Real [or, that it is the Truth]." Here Shabistari begins a rather long exegesis on the cosmos using the Ptolemaic model of concentric spheres. He also introduces the zodiac and considers the value of astrology. The Ptolemaic model, considered accurate in the time of Shabistari, happens to make an ideal working metaphor for the relationship between humanity, the cosmos, and God. He ends the section by expressing the same wonder that any scientist of our own day might feel when faced by the vastness and incomprehensibility of the universe.

**212**  The Throne is the level of existence where the Unmanifested surrounds both worlds, that is, this cosmos and the hereafter. The Prophet has said: "The earth of Heaven is the Footstool and the sky of Heaven is the Throne of the Merciful and rivers flow from that earth."

**213** There is a *ḥadīth* that "The heart of the faithful is the Throne of the Merciful." In other words, just as there is a cosmic Throne, It is mirrored within the heart of the Sufi.

**216** The completed Sufi is the microcosmic manifestation of the Real and the firmament circumscribes the Sufi just as people circumambulate the holy Ka'ba at Mecca.

**232** 'Knots' are the points at which the moon's orbit crosses the ecliptic. The moon's orbit north of the ecliptic is known as the 'head' (of the dragon) and that south of the ecliptic is called the 'tail.'

**258** Koran 17:44.

**259** The mother of the natural world has as father the Universal Intellect, also a mother as the Universal Soul. Adam, who is father to the human race, is also the mother of Eve, giving birth to her from his body.

**263** Darkness and ignorance seem opposite to truth and light; yet light requires a screen against which it can be reflected. Lahiji points out that man's qualities of darkness and ignorance are necessary to make him the microcosm.

**277** The Names are the qualities of God that sustain our world. Lists of the Names generally present them as ninety-nine in number.

**283** Lahiji comments here that the first relationship that the Essence has to the created world is Knowledge [meaning the Real's knowledge in Itself of the *a'yān thābita,* the fixed essences of all created things]. Next comes Life because without life there would be no forms. The seven Beautiful Names of Power, Knowledge, Will, Hearing, Seeing, Life, and Speaking, are called Essential Names. They and an eighth, Subsisting, manifest in the human being because the human is a mirror of the Real. In his own essence, the human is essentially of nonbeing, yet he becomes a locus of manifestation for these Names of the Real.

**284** This is a mystical interpretation of Koran 57:3. The First and the Last along with the Hidden and the Apparent are four more of the Names of God. Lahiji comments that man is First in that he is the reason for creation. He is last since he is last to appear. He is Hidden in that his inward essence is a mirror of the Real, and he is Apparent as a form in which manifest the Names.

**286** The bewilderment is mystical perplexity experienced by Sufis who have transcended forms through the proper contemplation of the Real "in the horizons and in their souls," and for whom Allah "becomes his hearing and his seeing." This discussion of contemplation ends where the First is one with the Last.

**291** Accidents [*a'rāḍ*] are phenomena, in other words, unreal and temporary manifestations which emanate from the Essence of Being. Lahiji writes that Absolute Being is the lamp, the world the niche, and that individual created things (as immutable entities) are like the patterned openings in the lamp projecting the illusion of multiplicity. (Koran 24:35).

**295** Lahiji explains that gnosis is represented by fatness, i.e. real and healthy knowledge; and speculation is compared to swelling, an indication of illness.

**296** The 'I' is the particularization of the Essence in that it is a locus for God's Self-manifestation.

**299** A literal translation is, "From the imaginary line writing the H of *huwiyyat,* two eyes will appear at the moment of vision." This couplet is an example of the subtle letter-play

found in several places in the *Gulshan-i rāz*. The ʜ is known
in Persian as the 'ʜ with two eyes.' It looks like the number eight turned on its side. The word *huwiyyat* stands for
identity in two senses: identity and Identity, or limited self
and Absolute Self. It literally means 'He-ness.' The two eyes,
which appear at the moment of vision, are those of self and
Self, phenomenal existence and Absolute Existence.

**300** This is an equivalent translation. The original indicates that when the ʜ of *hū* (a shortened form of the word
*huwiyyat,* meaning identity or individuality) is joined to the
ʜ in the word Allah, the latter being a different ʜ which is
nearly a circle, the duality of the first ʜ is absorbed in the
unity of the second. The word *hū* is also understood at all
times by the mystic to refer to God, and is invoked while
focusing on the "ʜ" sound of the outgoing breath. The last
two couplets refer to a Sufi exercise whose result can be a
theophany in the mystic's consciousness and a "passing away"
(*fanāʾ*) of worldly qualities.

**301** Pure Being is Heaven in that it possesses only the qualities of goodness, sweetness, purity, and the like. Phenomena
are like Hell because they have no inherent goodness of their
own and are devoid of the light of Being. The 'I' in between
is the soul which can manifest either Being or lack of It. For
this reason, this 'I' is called the *barzakh,* which means an
isthmus or an interworld.

**304** The *Kaʿba* is the name of the primary temple of Islam
located at Mecca in present-day Saudi Arabia.

**305** The "speck in the eye," also translates as "the dot on the
*ʿain,*" referring to an Arabic letter which by the addition of
a dot becomes the letter *ghain,* another letter that stands
for *ghubār,* meaning dust, fog, impurity, and also for *ghair,*

what is other than God. When, through Sufi exercises, the consciousness transcends the phenomenal world, it leaves the dotless *'ain,* meaning the eye which now sees clearly because the impurity has been removed.

**307** Line one of the couplet says literally, "to transcend the *Ha* of *Huwiyyat.*" This is an equivalent translation that catches some of the meanings inherent in the original. Please refer to the notes on couplet 299. This, in one sense, is the sound of the outgoing breath, representing *Hu* or *Huwiyyat,* the Divine Essence. Trancending it means that one is, while in meditation, merged with the Divine Presence and beyond the confines of personal identity. The second couplet refers to transcending the illusory 'existence' which is this world. The prophet Muhammad said in this connection: "Die before you die." When this takes place, one may find oneself removed from the world of phenomenal existence.

**315** Lahiji gives a poem to clarify this section from which I quote four lines which refer to the *dhikr* of "There is no god but Allah":

> *If you want to unveil the meaning of this,*
> *Strike other than God with the sword of 'no.'*
> *After negating the created, affirm the Real,*
> *That you may drown in the ocean of the Real's Essence.*

**317** This "Spirit blown" is the *rūḥ-i ezafi,* the Spirit which is from God (Koran 32:9, 15:29, 38:72).

**326** According to Lahiji, attraction means direct spiritual experience not mediated by reason, whereas the reflection of reason (which is the reflection or image of direct spiritual experience) does occur with the help of the intellect.

**328** The Faith of Certainty is beyond opinion or supposition. It is a mystical experience of the Real in the heart and the intellect. In the spiritual heart this is experienced as a bewildering attraction and in the intellect as certain gnosis of the Real. Lahiji writes, "The seeker traveling toward the Real by way of the light of mystical attraction or by means of certain reason, which is far from doubt and opinion, finds his way to certain faith and becomes a true worshiper, and that which is promised by prophets and saints manifests through an evident spiritual light or by the proof of witnessing so that imitation and doubt lift from in front of him."

**330** Repentance is not merely religious remorse but is a stage in the process of becoming a Sufi. *Tawba,* the word for repentance, means 'turning back,' in this case from the lower self, known as the *nafs-i ammāra*. This 'self' is the usual one ordinary people know. It is self-centered, fearful, covetous, contentious and proud. It is not considered to be the core of a human being, in the Sufi view. Repentance is a stage in which the mystic turns away from the insatiable appetites of this 'self' and seeks closeness to God.

**331** The mystic who has thus purified him/herself from the effects of self-love, greed, anger, jealousy, and lust will, according to Lahiji, experience the Divine Presence, an experience which is here likened to rising into the Heavens.

**332** That is, he is firm in his determination to turn away from his undesirable characteristics and keep his focus upon the Real.

**333** *Tawakkul,* or trust, is an elevated stage for the mystic where he or she is aware that all actions originate with the Real, and for that reason always has 'trust' in God.

**334** He enters through the highest gate, that is, the gate of Heaven since he or she now experiences Heaven on earth within the spiritual heart. This is because any wish of God is delightful to the mystic whether it is a manifestation of God's love or His wrath.

**335** Having abandoned his own knowledge means that he has passed away in the knowledge of God, which is far superior to personal knowledge. His state becomes like that of Jesus who possessed the 'Greatest Name,' a name of God by which Jesus performed miracles.

**336** Giving his existence over to plunder means that he dies completely to himself within God. The *mi'rāj* is the prophet Muhammad's miraculous ascension into the heavens where he reached a place so close to God that even the angel Gabriel could not follow. This is the final stage for the mystic, called *baqā'*, subsistence in God.

**338** This line refers to a *ḥadīth* of the Prophet in which he reports, "I have a time with God which neither angel nor prophet can strive after with me." This is where the farthest point of manifestation joins with the First, where the drop joins with the Sea.

**339** In Islam, the notion of *walāyat*, or sainthood, is a relationship of friendship with God. *Walī* means friend. A prophet of God has a specific mission that requires his 'friendship' to be openly manifested and can include the demonstration of true miracles to make the necessary impression on his following. A prophet, meanwhile, retains his private friendship with God, which has the pleasures of intimacy.

**340** The *walī*, or friend of God, who does not have a prophetic mission, rarely shows signs of miracles even if he or she is capable of them. The *walī*'s real miracle is his or her intimacy with God.

**342** Koran 3:31.

**345** After the annihilation in Unity and the drunkenness of that state, there is a further state in which the saint is once again sober and compelled to follow the religious requirements just like at the beginning of the journey.

After cutting across the distance between the Divine and Creation, the Completed Man is made the earthly representative of God.

**348** *Baqā'*, subsistence in God, is the highest state that a mystic can attain. In it, the soul of the mystic is always experiencing God. This occurs after the process of *fanā'*, annihilation in God, which is an extinguishing of the self of the mystic. These two important words refer to stages at the end of the mystic's journey, but can also be used to describe moments of the same experiences.

**356** A novice in the Sufi way must keep to the religious Sharia, or Law, represented by the shell. If that shell is opened too early, his mystical experiences will come to naught. If his or her mystical experiences are guided by the Law (the standards for obedience, humility, restraint, purity, honesty, generosity and the like), they will ripen to a state that transcends the Law, going to its Source.

**359** In the situation referred to in the preceding couplet, the mystic has transcended the normal states of awareness through ecstatic communion with God and never becomes 'normal' again. It is held that such a mystic is not bound by the religious Law since he or she is generally insensible to this material realm. In another case, the Real shines into the heart of such a mystic, and his moral and mystical perfection will be such that other individuals will be drawn to the Real through his guidance.

**363** The circle is often used by Shabistari to represent the arc of descent from Unity into multiplicity and the re-ascent of the completed human to the plane of Unity.

**367** The Seal of the Prophets is Muhammad, considered the bearer of the final revelation.

**369** The Seal of the Saints is thought to be the Mahdi, a blessed individual who will come near the end of the world just before the return of Jesus. Lahiji explains that the historical Muhammad is the outward [*ẓāhir*] manifestation of the Muhammadan Reality, the light of all prophecy and sainthood pre-existing our cosmos. The Mahdi is to manifest the inward [*bāṭin*] potential of the Muhammadan Reality.

**377** By analogy, shadows represent variations of the pure message of the Prophet Muhammad, variations that leave room for a more perfect prophecy. It is thought in Islam that Muhammad was created before all of the other prophets even though he appeared last to mankind.

**380** Koran 11:112.

**382** The *qibla* is the indicator of the direction of the holy temple at Mecca towards which all Muslims pray. The way of Muhammad is a middle and balanced way between form and spirit, rejecting neither but finding balance between them. The balance is also between *tanzīh,* trancendence, and *tashbīh,* immanence.

**400** Ardent devotion is given here for *nawāfil,* a technical term meaning any prayer, fasting, or devotion beyond what is required in Islam. The second line reads "with the *lā* of *nafy,*" meaning the "no of negation." This is in reference to the exercise of repeating "*lā ilāha illa Allāh,*" (There is no god [reality] except for Allah), which is used to clear all thoughts and images that sustain notions of 'I' and prevent the seeker from reaching God.

**405** The "evil of the Whisperer" refers to internal chatter, keeping people at a level of attachment and baseness. In Islam, these are attributed to *djinn* and to Satan, the manifestation of non-surrender to His Will. See Koran 114:4.

**407** According to Lahiji, the first purification is the ablution of the body, which purifies the worshiper for prayer. The second is also a purification to precede worship, that of sin or the voice to sin within the worshiper. These two purifications, he says, are normal for people who pray, but the mystic must further purify him/herself. Third is the work on oneself that removes the influence of bad habits such as improper morals and ethics that have become habitual. The last purification is of the 'secret,' which is none other than the mystic's heart, from self-identity, and from anything other than God.

**410** A *ḥadīth* of Muhammad goes, "In this world of yours, women and perfume have been made dear to me; and the delight of my eyes is in the ritual prayer."

**417** Koran 7:172. This is a widely quoted verse known as the covenant of *alast.*

**419** Lahiji writes that this is the script of *al-aʿyān al-thābita,* the immutable essences.

**423** Look at the Attributes of God in the world and come to know of Him what you can here, that after this life you may have a way of knowing Him. Otherwise, you will be miserable. This also refers to the subject brought up in question two, namely that it is important to understand the attributes of God first, here in this world, by using the senses and the capacity for reflection. After this, one may travel within oneself to know the Essence through Its effects.

**424** A reference to the Koran (28:56) in which God tells the Prophet that he cannot guide whom he loves but that God guides whomever He wants. Thus, if you do not attain to knowledge of the Essence, do not grieve, since this has been predetermined for you.

**431** Lahiji writes that the special faculty is *ʿishq*, meaning spiritual love and attraction. The faculty has been placed in spirit and body. The mental negation of other than God, and the renunciation of the desires of the body, produces the fire of *ʿishq* which illuminates the two worlds. Independently they do not produce the same effect just as a spark is not produced without both flint and steel.

**438** Koran 17:44.

**439** *Ḥallāj* means a cotton-carder.

**442** This refers to the story of Moses' meeting with God (Koran 28:30), and his hearing God speak through the burning bush.

**444** In other words, if you say "I am God," or, "I am He," this implies the duality of 'I' and 'He.' By saying, "I am the Real," Hallaj avoids this duality.

**449** Incarnation or union implies two separate absolutes. These views are denied by Shabistari throughout the *Gulshan-i rāz*. He questions dualistic views found in Christianity, Hinduism, and some Sufism.

**460** This statement, a quote from Muslim interpreters of Greek philosophy, refers to one of several philosophical views that were held at this time concerning substance and accident. In the view being questioned, substance is seen to be compounded of accidents. Shabistari makes fun of this view by asking, if accidents are perishable, what can be thought of that which is compounded of them?

**469** It is not the creature, or created aspect of an individual that is united with the Real. Rather this phenomenal aspect lifts away and the Real is with Itself. The enlightened sage never says that the creature is united with the Real but rather that the illusion of the creature's 'existence' disappears.

**473** The creature's existence is only within the Knowledge of the Real, as an immutable entity [*'ayn thābit*]. For this reason, Shabistari describes the creature as ephemeral, powerless, and motionless. The seeming existence, power and motion in creatures are all Attributes of the Real manifesting within the nonbeing of the immutable entity.

**490** The "rational soul," or "speaking soul" [*nafs-i guya*], is what makes a person human.

**498** "Finally the Completed Person," is used because his or her comprehensive mirror-consciousness is the aim and the spirit of the cosmos.

**500** The Universal Intellect and the Universal Soul are the first manifestations of Divinity in the process of bringing about our cosmos.

These definitions are borrowed from Greek thought, but correspond to the Koranic "Pen" and "Tablet."

**502** Koran 10:24.

**508** Creatures other than human beings are thought to manifest the Attributes of the Real in a partial way. All creatures are linked to the comprehensive manifestation, which is the Completed Human. For this reason, Shabistari directs seekers to study aspects of themselves in the rest of creation.

**510** The Necessary is God, who exists forever. The contingent means the phenomena of His creation which are transient.

**517** Once the mystic truly sets out on the Way, and attains to some experience of Self-manifestation, he or she is no longer in need of prodding since mystical experience is compelling enough to make it the most important pursuit in life. Worldly people may need the threat of hell's punishment and the promise of Heaven, but the mystic is sustained by a direct contact with God.

**526** Muslim culture came into contact with a number of older religions during its expansion across Asia. Zoroastrianism was already two thousand years old and had undergone a substantial degeneration from the influence of Manichaeism. The criticism leveled here against Zoroastrianism (or a decayed version of it) is that the individual is considered to have personal will and control over events. This implies a will in an individual that is separate from God's. Sufism is a teaching of Absolute Unity, whose viewpoint does not accept such duality in existence.

**527** By analogy, how does the image in a mirror claim, "I am a doer?" If the Real Doer is visualized as Himself and His mirror, then what can be said about the doing of the image? If the image then claims, "Then, I am the same as the Doer," this does not take into account the condition of the reflectivity of the mirror. It may be perfectly polished and it may be nearly rusted over. And yet, elsewhere, Shabistari emphasizes the need to strive. This paradox is not intended to be worked out intellectually. There is a macrocosmic reality that the mystic can come to know which is different from the partial viewpoint of the microcosm which has not transcended its limited knowledge. The advice to the seeker is always to strive, to purify him or herself, and this advice implies a qualified free will. At the microcosmic level, this is effectively true.

**532** Koran 12:21. The last few verses are intended to demonstrate the lack of any true free will in creation. While man often thinks that he can determine his future, Shabistari asks the question as to how many of his wishes he actually achieves, and shows that man has no real control. In this couplet, he points out that any attainment, even spiritual (as the word used here, *marātib,* implies attainment of spiritual states) is completely subject to the will of God.

**533** The Sufis hold that all of creation, including human beings' actions, was created before manifestation in physical form. The special role of the human, according to Lahiji, is to act as a complete mirror for God's Names, Effects, and Actions.

**541** This line refers to Satan.

**543** The last two lines refer to Adam who sinned but came to a state of purity nonetheless. The comparison is to Satan's millennia of obedience resulting only in his rejection by God, whose inscrutable plan can never be understood by us. What Shabistari finds strangest of all, according to Lahiji, is that man became even more dear to God because Satan would not bow to Adam when the angels were told to do so. This helped to make Adam the 'chosen' and increased God's mercy toward him. Satan became especially accursed not only for disobeying God's command, but for tempting Adam.

**546**  Abu Jahl was the Prophet Muhammad's persistent antagonist and a great source of trouble to him during his early mission at Mecca.

**552**  Shabistari explores the paradox of how man can be held responsible for his actions if he has no real will, and all of his actions have been determined by God from the beginning. Lahiji writes that this also proves that God's work cannot be grasped by the intellect.

**554**  The word employed is *faḍl*, which means grace, favor, and learning.

**571**  The knowledge of the Names is knowledge of the Attributes of God. These Names, identifying the qualities of God acting within His manifestations including our world, are ninety-nine in number but interact, making the possibilities almost limitless. Knowledge of the Names allows the seeker a deep understanding of God's workings, but this is not knowledge of the Essence of God, which is transcendent and self-subsistent.

**584**  The East represents spirituality. The mystic turns toward the metaphysical East, source of the spiritual sun. The worldly follow the West, the phenomena which the sun makes appear to exist.

**588**  In most parts of the Islamic world, dogs are not allowed into homes and they usually lack gentle contact with people. Consequently, they are fierce, hungry, covetous and territorial.

**593**  Koran 41:53.

**594**  Justice comes ahead of the other virtues because it represents the wise directing of a person's actions [*'amal*], and represents the proper mean, or middle way, between the extremes found in thinking and behavior.

**596** The third person pronoun used in Persian is neutral. I have occasionally chosen to translate it as the feminine since, although written works were in Shabistari's time addressed almost entirely to a male audience, there were and are many women who follow the Sufi way. In this couplet, wisdom is seen as the middle way between deceit and foolishness, both of which are considered undesirable.

**597** *'Iffa* is the chastity of Islam, which allows for normal expression of sexual desire within a licit relationship, and is considered a blessing to spiritual work rather than the hazard supposed by monastic tradition. On the contrary, Sufism regards the monastic traditions as being in danger of creating individuals obsessed with sexuality or in such a state of sexual abatement as to reduce the energy and integration of real spirituality in daily life. *'Iffa* is the mean, and wantonness and abatement are undesirable extremes.

**598** Courage is the mean between cowardice and impetuosity. It allows one to effect the other virtues of justice, chastity and wisdom. It can be directed toward one's own weaknesses and toward the unjust of the world.

**601** A reference to one of the lines in the *fātiḥa*, the opening prayer of Islam, said by Muslims many times each day. In it, the worshiper asks Allah to show the "straight way," or correct approach, to Him.

**604** Shabistari does not identify the seven gates to Hell mentioned in the Koran (15:44), but Lahiji infers from the passage that the gates are related to deviations from each of the four means of the excellent virtues: cruelty; deceit and foolishness; wantonness and rejection of the natural order (monasticism); impetuosity and cowardice. Note that only one deviation is counted against justice, that is cruelty. Fatalism is not counted as the other extreme because from the Sufi point of view, struggling against events is not practiced. In the place of struggle, 'spiritual poverty' [*faqr*] is practiced and the Sufi accepts the blows of fate.

**608** The compound being referred to is the body which, through unification of its parts, becomes a separate whole.

**609** Shabistari is referring to the link of Spirit which appears in the body and Rational Soul which have joined. Spirit is not made up of them, nor limited by them.

**619** The Universal Soul is the second emanation of Divinity both in Neoplatonism and Sufism. The human soul has been so created that it is affected by the Names of Allah, which permeate all of the elements of our earth, and shape them into beautiful forms. Though physical, they are symbols full of meaning because of their pure origin.

**630** Mystics of all traditions point the seeker toward spiritual rather than physical beauty. Most agree, however, that God's beauty also manifests in the physical world. Lahiji comments on this passage: "The attraction of a lover toward a beauty is not carnal desire. On the contrary, only God acts upon creation and it is God which attracts hearts, even when this isn't clear, since He is manifesting under His name of Majesty."

**632** In this reply, Shabistari tackles the doctrine of 'the oneness of Being' [*waḥdat al-wujūd*] from another angle. In the realm of appearances, including our world, Real Being is inherent in all things, though concealed. Lahiji writes, "The existent [*mawjūd*] is Being [*wujūd*] plus individual form [*ta'ayyun*]." So Being can, from this context, be seen to be a part of any existent thing even though this Part is greater than the seeming whole.

**639** "Accidents" are phenomena. The word I have translated as "compounded" [*ijtimāʿī*] is a term meaning conjunction, which is in part, perishable. When the part perishes, the compound also perishes.

**645** Koran 79:34. It is the experience of Sufis that creation oscillates at each moment between existence and non-existence. Shabistari explains that this is not the same as God's promise that the universe will be destroyed by Him at the end of time, and then recreated as the Resurrection.

**664** Koran 20:106.

**667** Koran 55:26.

**675** When manifestations, here meaning humanity, are in conformity with the Manifest, a conformity which is God's intention for them, then in the First appears what is in the Last. The First is undelimited Being which is made apparent in the Last, humanity cleared of individual determinations. Lahiji offers the simile of a mirror which, when cleaned and polished, possesses a reflectivity which is in conformity with what is being reflected.

**676** *Al-Bāqī,* the Enduring, is one of Allah's ninety-nine names. God is what endures or remains in the consciousness of mystics who have completely annihilated their personal existence. This verse is pointing out that *baqā'* is evidence of, and belongs to, real Being. It is only found in creation to the extent that real Being is inherent in a creature. Even though the Remaining is a word used for Being, that Being manifests in the limitless loci of manifestation of this world.

**685** Koran 86:9.

**687**  The three natures are inanimate/insensible, animate/sensible, and intelligent.

**694**  Koran 76:21.

**703**  The phoenix ['anqā'], is used as a metaphor for the forms of the world because its plumage contains the colors found in all of the birds of the world.

**712**  The chameleon [būqalamūn], is also the word for a black and white feathered bird, whose colors symbolize being and nonbeing.

**736**  Real mystics become so through revelations experienced as 'gifts' or special, often rapturous, states of mind or through the intuitive experience of certainty. These states are antithetical to boasting and idle speculation.

**741**  The word "Witness" [shāhid] is used by Sufis to mean a self-disclosure of God. Mystics use this word to describe a theophanic appearance, whether as a spiritual unfolding in the mystic's heart, or as the beauty of a lovely person. A beautiful person is considered a "Witness" because his or her beauty offers evidentiary proof of the Beauty and Presence of the Real. *Shahidbazi* means 'the play of gazing at a beloved' while striving for the Essential beauty inherent in the physical beauty. Sufis use this terminology to emphasize the interactive, reflective nature of the contact between the Real, His beautiful creation, and the mystic. The couplet means that one should use the theophany of earthly beauty to make a leap to the *'ālam-i ma'ānī,* the World of Meanings.

**747**  In other words, the rest of creation burns in envy at Her attention to humanity.

**755**(1)  Koran 16:77.

**755**(2)  Koran 15:19 and 38:72.

**759** Koran 20:39.

**760** The curls and tresses represent the multiplicity of veils between the lover and the Unique Real, which is due to the action of the Divine Names. The Beloved is often portrayed combing Her hair over Her face, the latter representing the Essence of the Real, which is occasionally sensed through the fragrant locks.

**773** Human nature carries the fragrance of her locks, meaning the predisposition to be affected by all the divine Names and their qualities and effects. In the next couplets, Shabistari indicates that this is the reason why we are never at rest, and why spiritual progress in achieving detachment from the world of form is so difficult.

**779** The World of Spirits is the Abode of Eternal Life because, even after the death of material bodies, their original spiritual identities remain undying in the World of Spirits. This reality is the basis for the afterlife.

**780** Her locks, as the external manifestations of Reality, make day into night. That is, the seeker should extinguish their visibility and apparent reality with the night of self-annihilation.

**781** Khidr is the hidden guide of the Sufis. He is teacher to such figures as Moses and Ibn al-ʿArabi. His cloak is a luminescent green color.

**784** Shabistari says here that he is at the stage of seeing God within all the determinations of creation whereas the average person may see that the individual determinations belong to God.

**785** The verses referred to are those of the *fātiḥa,* the opening chapter of the Koran.

787 With the down pictured as a verdant meadow with its spring of life, still water becomes a mirror to the seeker's Heart as in the verse: "His Throne is on the water" (Koran 11:7).

788 This point represents the unity of the Essence, which surrounds all manifested possibility.

792 Though the human Heart was created as a reflection of the Real, it suffers since the only resolution for this Heart's painful existence is to give way to the Unity implicit in its creation.

796 Shabistari marvels at the varied states of the Heart, the spiritual organ of perception, whose word root in Arabic includes the concept of constant change. If the mole representing Unity is reflected in the Heart, shouldn't the Heart experience only unity? The answer is that the Heart can experience Unity as well as the manifestations emanating from the Real's Names.

810 "The wine that will release you from self" is the state which arises in a mystic through one-pointed attention on God. When the structure of self-regard gives way, a state of inner vastness and radiance is uncovered.

813 Koran 76:21.

815 Emptying one's self of self-importance is better than thinking of one's own goodness. Shabistari warns here that hypocrisy is the great danger of religion.

816 "Veils of darkness" represent overt sins such as immorality and other violations of religious law. Shabistari warns that these are far less dangerous than "veils of light," i.e. sins of hypocritical religious vanities.

**821** The Universal Soul gives rise to our physical cosmos. It "wears the ring of a slave" because all things that arise within creation inwardly agitate to rejoin their Origin, represented by wine and wine-drinking.

**863** An idol does not only mean a statue or image of deity such as a crucifix or a statue of the Buddha. Idolatry is the focus of attention onto an intermediary, and is condemned in orthodox religion because it pulls the worshiper from the awareness of the transcendence of God. Nevertheless, Sufis often defend idolatry as a means to an end. Human beauty, for example, is regarded as borrowed from the Real and therefore sacred as such. It allows one to understand beauty in general and can lead to understanding beauty beyond form. In the special states where the unity of immanent and transcendent is experienced, an idol is seen as a Self-manifestation of the Real.

**873** 'True denial' is the denial and hiding of oneself in God. Ordinary and sinful denial and infidelity is the hiding of God within oneself.

**875** Koran 17:44.

**876** Koran 6:91.

**880** Koran 67:3.

**883** Koran 2:40. This is known as the pledge of *alast*.

**889** Psychic wonders like telepathy can be experienced by someone astray or unacquainted with the mystic Way. Shabistari warns that they are not, in themselves, a mark of relevant attainment. Only closeness to God is true attainment.

**901** Shabistari is here denouncing those false teachers who always abound and whose seeming success is based on a pious appearance. In his time, as in some of contemporary

Islamic culture, a long beard represented piety. He pokes fun at this by putting a beard on a donkey.

**903** Dajjal is the Antichrist predicted to come near the end of the world. Ignorant so-called 'Sufis' represent his ignorance in the meantime.

**904** Jassas spies on people to ascertain their weaknesses. This donkey is being compared to false students of these so-called 'teachers.'

**911** This is a reference to a story in the Koran, in which Moses is surprised by some of the actions of God's great saint Khidr, including the killing of a boy alluded to here.

**919** Tying the Christian belt means his resolution both to live up to the ethics of the religious law and to distinguish himself from the mere pretenders who appear as pious men.

**941** Koran 23:101.

**956** The *ḥanīf* is the archetypal mystic who is one with God. He or she is to be found across time and cultures. Uwais al-Qarani, a saint in the time of Muhammad, was such a person.

**964** Shabistari refers to the literal meaning of Muslim: one surrendered to God.

**969** Lahiji comments that the Christian youth represents the perfect spiritual guide who is beyond being concerned about what people think, and consequently seems to be a heretic to the uninitiated. The idol represents the Real manifesting through the Perfect Human who is the locus of the theophanies of the comprehensive Unity of the Essence of the Real.

**1004** *Maḥmūd,* Shabistari's given name, means "worthy of praise."